CW00394451

# TWILIGHT OF THE GODS

A Swedish Waffen-SS Volunteer's
Experiences with the 11th SS Panzergrenadier
Division Nordland, Eastern Front 1944-45

Edited by

## Thorolf Hillblad

Translated by Jackie Logan with the assistance of Thorolf Hillblad

Helion & Company

Helion & Company Limited
26 Willow Road
Solihull
West Midlands
B91 1UE
England
Tel. 0121 705 3393
Fax 0121 711 4075
Email: publishing@helion.co.uk
Website: http://www.helion.co.uk

Published by Helion & Company Limited 2004

Designed and typeset by Helion & Company Limited, Solihull, West Midlands
Cover designed by Bookcraft Limited, Stroud, Gloucestershire
Printed by The Cromwell Press, Trowbridge, Wiltshire

Originally published with the title *Ragnarok* © Thorolf Hillblad 1945
This corrected and revised English edition © Thorolf Hillblad 2002, published under license
by Helion & Company Limited

ISBN 1 874622 16 7

British Library Cataloguing-in-Publication Data.
A catalogue record for this book is available from the British Library.

All photographs and illustrations, including those appearing on the dustjacket, appear courtesy
of Erik Norling.

For details of other military history titles published by Helion & Company contact the above
address, or visit our website: http://www.helion.co.uk.

We always welcome receiving book proposals from prospective authors.

# Contents

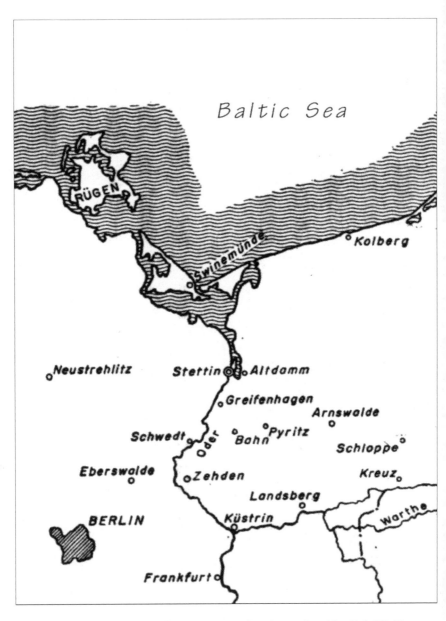

Map showing the area of the majority of exploits related by Erik Wallin,
including Stettin, Altdamm, Schwedt, Küstrin, and of course, Berlin.

# Foreword

At the end of World War II, the Nuremberg war tribunal sentenced the Waffen SS, possibly the finest fighting force the world has seen since Leonidas and his Spartans at Thermopylae, the bravest of the brave, collectively as war criminals. As an ex-Waffen SS volunteer, well aware of the strong discipline and high morale of these exceptional warriors, originally all volunteers, I decided to write down the experiences of some Swedish SS comrades in the fight against the Red Army.

My first interviewee was Erik (Jerka) Wallin from Stockholm. In late 1945 he had just been released from a Swedish prison where he had served a few months for the 'theft' of his Swedish army uniform. Before crossing the border to join the Waffen SS he had wrapped it in a neat parcel, which somehow had gone astray. During the war it was no crime in Sweden to join the German or Finnish forces against the Soviet Union. After the war, however, the Swedish authorities felt embarrassed about their past neutrality and became anxious to establish good terms with Sweden's large neighbour in the east. So 'Jerka' had to go to jail as an expression of Sweden's new-found friendliness with the Soviet Union.

Erik's neighbours in prison were hard-boiled violent repeat criminals. Being 'politically correct' criminals, it was hard for them to tolerate this disgusting war criminal in their cosy Swedish prison, equipped with all modern conveniences. Erik had been quite a good amateur boxer, but he hadn't a chance when they made it a habit to collectively beat him up, with the wardens as onlookers.

He had been through the war up to the fall of Berlin, with a very short stint as a Red Army POW. It turned out that his experiences gave enough material for this book, so I forgot about further interviews. He visited me every evening, and between cups of coffee and cigarettes he talked 'til late in the night, while I took down the details. Jerka's tale is not a continuous chronological description of his participation in the last six months of the Second World War, rather some episodes in the tremendous battles fought during those days.

As a marked man - after the war Sweden was no longer neutral - I was jobless, so in daytime I typed what he had told me the night before. I was in a bit of a hurry, because the profit from the sale of the book was to cover the debts of our weekly paper *Den Svenske*, the finances of which

5

were in terrible shape. In two weeks the job was finished. We printed only one edition, which was sold out within a few weeks. It did not occur to us to print a second edition, because the first one had already solved our financial problems. In 1947 a German translation was published in Argentina where thousands of SS men - Dutch, French, Belgian, Scandinavian, and of course German - had sought refuge. In the mid 1990's - after 50 years! - pirate editions started appearing in Scandinavia and Germany. So, some of the book contents may be worth reading ...

Erik Wallin continued his eventful life in various countries - like many comrades, he became restless - some rather exotic, such as Morocco and Afghanistan. He met many interesting people and even became friendly with the last (or latest?) King of Afghanistan, Zahir Shah, who has lately enjoyed some publicity with his return to Kabul. Zahir Shah liked to listen to Jerka's war escapades. Among other notables Erik met was Ilya' Ehrenburg, Stalins court jester, one of the few intimates of the Red Tsar to survive Stalin's 'clear-outs'. Ilya and Jerka must have had some interesting things to tell each other ... In later years, Erik and I used to meet in Stockholm for a few days once a year, reminiscing over *bratwurst, sauerkraut, 'Kommisbrot* and beer. By then I had lived in Argentina for almost fifty years, a very, very different country. Erik's 'light' went out one evening at a get-together of Division Nordland veterans in Germany. It happened fast, as so many things in his life did!

Thorolf Nilsson Hillblad
Coeur d' Alene, Idaho, 2002

*Unsere Ehre heisst Treue*
"Our honour is our unbreakable loyalty"
(motto of the Waffen-SS)

*Together with Army Group North, which consisted of the 16th and 18th armies, III (Germanic) Panzerkorps under SS-Obergruppenführer Felix Steiner was cut off from the other German forces, in Courland. The seaport of Libau was of vital importance for the encircled forces. From the middle of October 1944 Steiner's Panzerkorps, which consisted of the 11th SS Panzergrenadier Division 'Nordland', and the 23rd SS Panzergrenadier Division 'Nederland', held the front at Preekuln – Purmsati – Skuodas.*

*The main line of defence ran along the railway, through the ruins of Purmsati and the village of Bunkas. On one side of the railway tracks lay the SS soldiers, and on the other, the Red Army. About 1 kilometre north of Purmsati lay the village of Bunkas. At times it was very cold – temperatures below 30°C were recorded.*

## 1

# New Year's Eve 1944–1945

We sat round the roughly-made bunker table playing cards, and listening to the front's New Year radio appeals from the highest commanders of the different services. We could also tune in to Christmas music. The bunker had been decorated, as well as we could, on Christmas Eve. There was a Christmas tree, fresh spruce-twigs, tinsel, and small items we had received in the recent field-post parcels. By New Year's Eve it was still looking as homely as it could in a temporary underground bunker. Soldiers' rough, chapped and frozen hands had tenderly and carefully conjured up this Christmas treasure for all to share. We still cared for such in the days between Christmas and New Year.

On the stove were some canteens with steaming *Glogg,* our Nordic version of English mulled and spiced wine. Every now and then each man took a mouthful from one of the canteens, for once carefully cleaned. We had enjoyed smoking lots of the generously distributed Christmas cigarettes, from field-post parcels that had also contained sweets and biscuits. The playing cards regularly slammed down on the rough table. Quiet humming to the melodies on the radio was only occasionally interrupted by some racy comment on the game, or by a violent snore from one of the comrades of the relief guard sleeping on the floor, the exhausted sleep of a frontline soldier.

There was a jarring signal from the field-telephone. It was the company commander. He wanted to speak to me about a planned fire correction for the next day. Our mortar fire was to be aimed at a new target in the enemy positions. He ordered me to go to our outpost closest to the enemy, outside the village, to try to get a general view of the area that my mortars would fire on in the morning.

One of my comrades took over my cards. I put on the snow camouflage overall, took the ammo-pouch for the submachine-gun and put the white-painted steel helmet on my head. On the way out, I took a generous swig of *Glogg* from my canteen on the stove as I looked around the bunker. Suddenly, it seemed so warm, cozy and full of comfort, even with its stamped-down earth floor. On the partially-boarded, black-brown, damp walls fluttered the shadows of the men around the radio, in the light of the Christmas candles. With my trusty MP40 submachine-gun under my arm, I nodded to the men at the table, shoved the white-frosted door open with my foot, and went out into the night.

The moon appeared from behind a silver-edged cloud and covered the entire surroundings in a dazzling bright light. In the reflected whiteness of the cold sparkling snow, all outlines appeared razor sharp. A group of trees, riddled by bullets and shells, with their splintered trunks and twisted network of branches, reminded me of grotesque figures in a fairy-tale about brownies and hobgoblins.

The village, or small town, or what once had been something like that, looked more ghostlike than usual. Out of the snow-covered piles of stone and rubble, where houses used to stand and where there were now neither houses nor streets, only solitary chimneys blackened by fire rose up here and there, missed by the Russian artillery and mortar-fire. In the snow-covered dead village, black holes irregularly dotted the ground among the ruins. They were the only traces of the day's Russian shelling. The artillery shells had made furrows, but where the rounds from the big 12cm mortars had hit, there were big round spots, with black splashes around them, spread out on the frozen ground.

No life was visible in the ruins. But if the alarm should go, warning of an enemy attack, swarms of 'creatures' would leap up among them, because under the ground, in the cellars of the damaged houses, there were soldiers everywhere. They were ready to run out into the trenches to meet the Bolsheviks with a deadly fire.

Such was the New Year's Eve of 1944–45 in Bunkas, the little 'nest' in Courland that had given us protection among its ruins from death out in the wide-open spaces of this vast landscape. Because of that it had become a link in the defence line that we soldiers called the HKL – *Hauptkampflinie*, or main line of defence - in the Courland bridgehead. Cut off from every connection with mainland Germany, we stood there ready to try to stop the violent assault from the east, from Asia.

After more than 3 years of struggle in the east, and 2 years of almost continuous retreat, our fighting spirit was still unbroken. We persevered under the hardest conditions. Every day, comrades faced death and destruction. The last physical energy and mental force was almost drained out of the common soldier, but our fighting spirit was still there. Our faith lay firmly in the final victory of the superior power of our weapons. Our trust in our own combat skill, against the barbaric masses from the east, was as strong as ever.

It was true that every day we heard on the radio, of the British and Americans pushing our comrades in the west ever harder and harder. Giant bomber 'armadas' every day and night threw their murderous cargo over German cities, obliterating lives and homes. But we knew that a significant part of the most vital German industries had gone below ground and were therefore invulnerable from the air. We knew that even better weapons would soon be mass-produced, and that the German forces in the west, just a few days before, had started a successful offensive in Belgium and Luxembourg. Soon, the terrible pressure of numerically superior forces would have to ease. We just needed some months of breathing space!

Then we would hit back with annihilating power, especially here in Courland. The 11th SS *Panzergrenadier* Division Nordland and the other troops in this isolated island of resistance had an extremely important mission. With our toughness and persistence against the furious assaults of the Red Army, we could offer a breathing space to the reserves, who were now being organised and freshly equipped in Germany.

I put out my dangerously gleaming cigarette against the doorway. The bunker with the mortar crew was situated about 300 metres behind the actual front line. The company commander's bunker was in the cellar of what once was the railway station. He had told me to come to him first, to get further instructions. In fact it was quite a distance to get there, but on the other hand I could feel safe from enemy observation almost all the way. I moved the ammo-pouch to the side, gripped the submachine-gun harder and went off. In passing, I kicked a dead, stiff, frozen rat that had disgustingly exposed front teeth. There were plenty of big, fat rats in Bunkas.

Many rude words had been spoken in Swedish, German, Danish, Norwegian, and later, most likely, in Russian and Mongolian tongues too, over the ruins in Bunkas. I did the same, as I made my way to the CO's bunker, stumbling over frozen bricks. Fortunately, I did not have to bother about the Russian snipers, who otherwise were very numerous in our sector. We only had to watch out for the artillery and the mortars! However, they seemed to be celebrating New Year's Eve in peace and quiet at that moment. With aching knees I approached a protecting wall, about 20 metres from the CO's bunker. Between the wall and the bunker entrance the distance was open and unprotected. During the previous day, Ivan had managed to take a small hillock on the other side of a low railway embankment. From there he could cover the open distance with his machine-gun fire. Crouching, I ran over the open space and reached the bunker door just as I heard machine-guns 'rattle'. With a nasty singing and whirring they hit the walls and piles of bricks. Further back in the ruins the bullets ricocheted up in the air.

Reporting to the company commander, who was playing chess at that moment, I was permitted to take a short rest in the welcome warmth. The company commander was my fellow countryman *SS-Obersturmführer* Hans-Gösta Pehrsson, 'GP'. The strong discipline, even in the daily work at the front, which only genuine comradeship between superior officers and their subordinates managed to maintain, gave the Waffen-SS part of its fighting power. Down here the men had made it, if possible, even more homely than in the mortar crew's bunker. A wall-runner saying „Egen härd är guld värd" ('Our hearth is worth gold'), which in some strange way had found its way out here to the furthest outpost in the east, contributed to the cosiness.

Without interrupting the chess game the commander gave me the orders. They concerned just that 'troublesome' machine-gun nest out there, which had to be wiped out. Our mortars had to make it a grave for any Red Army soldier who dared to go there. The company commander served me a drink from a bottle of Steinhäger schnapps – "for its good warmth," he said – and I went out to make my observations. A connecting trench led me to the two soldiers by their machine-gun in the outpost. Wild shooting was going on and I naturally, wondered what was happening.

"Oh, they are just firing in the sky over there, to celebrate New Year's Eve, and we have to answer."

By then the insane shooting-party had spread to the whole sector. Everywhere firearms crackled on both sides.

"Seems they are totally drunk on the other side," the machine-gunner said. "Listen to their brawling!"

On the other side of the railway embankment, only about 50 metres from our machine-gun nest, the Bolsheviks had their most advanced position, which was manned only at night. Sometimes they used to attack our guards by crawling across and throwing hand-grenades. In the daytime the position was empty.

Some sounds were heard that were rather unusual for ordinary nights at the front. Someone played a mouth organ, and we could hear the others talking quite loudly. After a while the firing became less intense and soon it ceased completely. Even the exhilarated Bolsheviks over there became silent. In peace and quiet I could make my observations and calculations for the next day.

The weather was on my side, because the clouds, which occasionally swept over the front line, covered me as I went to take a look at surroundings that were usually lit by the moon. The violently battered area was silent. The silence was only occasionally broken by the metallic sound of a weapon that hit some object, or by a hushed mumble from the enemy side. Not even the usual sounds of engines from supply columns, so common at night, nor the clattering sounds from tanks, could be heard. Only now and then a flare rose into the sky and for some moments threw a sharp light over the deserted and lacerated landscape. New Year's Eve at the front!

The beautiful scene kept me out there after I had carried out my orders. Generated by the stillness and the meaning of the Eve, a mood caught me as I was standing there in the trench, together with my two comrades. My thoughts began to wander. They were suddenly interrupted when from the Russian trench on the other side of the railway track I heard a raucous guttural Mongolian voice:

"Comrade, why are you so melancholy? Did you get cabbage soup for dinner today, again?"

The words came slowly, in terribly broken German, but in a conversational tone. In the calm, bright night they reached us as clearly as if the Russian were here, among us three, in the machine-gun nest. The machine-gunner grabbed my arm and we all looked at each other in amazement. For the first time, in three and a half years of war, we experienced a Bolshevik talking to us over no-man's-land. So bitter had been this struggle that it had never happened, as it had during the First World War, that the soldiers fighting each other had spoken across the trenches during a pause in the fighting.

As we recovered from the surprise, we started to laugh out loud, and the laughing spread to the other posts in the guard line, where they too had heard the Russian. The slow tone, the heavy accent and the mutual point about soldiers' food always having recurrent cabbage soup, had given a perfect comic effect. The machine-gunner beside me fired a joyful burst up into the sky and, for a few moments, the rattle of all automatic weapons in the neighbourhood rolled out over the wide-open spaces. Then it became quiet. We waited excitedly for what might come next.

"Why do you shoot, comrade?" asked the same voice from the Russian side.

"If you come over here and play the mouth organ for us, I will not shoot any more," said the machine-gunner.

We peered cautiously over. It could be a trick to make us feel safe. You never knew. The shrewdness of the Bolsheviks had often caused us inconvenience.

The night sky was now completely cloudless, and the intense, cold moonlight, strengthened by the reflective light of the gleaming snow, made the surroundings almost like daylight. All the guards nearby had heard what the two had said, and were now waiting for the Russian's answer, without relaxing their attention. From the other side an eager mumble was heard. It was obvious that the proposal from this side has been taken under consideration. Then it became quiet on the other side. Through the wide open doors of a freight car that had fallen over on the railway track between us and their 'nest,' I saw a head come up and stand out clearly against the gleaming white background. Then a pair of shoulders emerged and indeed, there came a Red Army soldier, in full view, struggling towards the railway embankment. Another two followed.

Having reached the car, the first one blew a few tunes on the mouth organ to convince us that the asked for music session had come. They made some completely unsuccessful attempts to climb the wrecked car. Obviously there was a lot of vodka splashing around in their stomachs. But after all, it was New Year's Eve only once a year. Even on our side the mood was quite good, thanks to the generous bestowal of Steinhäger, Korn, Stargarder Kümmelschnapps and wine, which we had received in the Christmas parcels. The drunken (to put it mildly) Bolsheviks gave up their attempts to climb into the car amid general laughter, and instead lined up in front of it, on our side.

The first tune was burdensome and melancholy, with capricious Russian twists and turns. Their faces were in the shadows, but I could clearly see the seams in their thickly padded tunics, which swelled over their broad, stocky figures. There was a sudden change to a more vivacious tune. It sounded like a Cossack dance. The second man at our machine-gun started to jump to the music, with both feet together, to get the cold out of his feet, but had to give it up because of the quickly increasing speed of the rhythm. In a wild crescendo the music stopped.

The Russian in the middle made an attempt at a deep bow and fell headlong. A howl of laughter was heard from the guards on both sides. With difficulty he worked his way up on to his feet again, apparently hurt by the heartless laughter. When the laughter had somewhat subsided, there came from the fourth soldier, in the Bolshevik outpost on the other side of the embankment, a dirty joke about private parts, that every veteran on our side understood without any problem. Then the snorting laughter rose like a surge over the open space again, and echoed back from the ruins behind us. It followed the three New Year's Eve musicians, as they arm-in-arm started their staggering retreat to the nest on the other side.

The company commander who had heard the jollification as he was standing outside his bunker, philosophising, came into the connecting trench with us to find out what was going on. Excited by the remarkable experience, all three of us started to tell him simultaneously about the Bolsheviks' New Year's idea. As he heard the astonishing story, he said, laughing and holding up his hands, "I have heard about such things, but that it should happen here, in a war with such a fanatical enemy and in front of us, the Waffen-SS, whom every faithful Bolshevik hates, sounds like a Scandinavian sailor's yarn." He shook his head thoughtfully. "I wonder what Ivan is up to. There must be something else behind this sudden cosiness."

He looked in the trench-mirror, turned it slowly in different directions, studied the terrain just in front of us and the ground closest behind the nearest enemy positions, and deliberated. "Damn it, men! Just keep your eyes and ears wide open!" He returned to his bunker.

The conversation over no-man's-land started again. We chatted about this and that. The subject of Christmas gifts came up. It was obvious that the Red Army soldiers had got some extra fare, too, despite the Soviet godlessness. Then an eager overbidding about the excellence of the received gifts started. When they enthusiastically described the fine contents of their parcels, we laughed, mildly indulgent, and knocked them flat with a full list of our own Christmas gifts, but we carefully improved a few grades of quality above what was real. The effect was noticeable.

But the Bolsheviks were tough. We had noticed that, during earlier engagements over the past three years. Even this time it seemed they did not want to give up, without trying a 'counter-attack.' After some mumbling they raised their voices over there and came again with renewed strength. But we saw through them. They went too far with their violent exaggerations, but it cannot be denied that they had improved their position. It began to seem like a 'dead heat!'

Then the final decision came fast and unexpectedly. An old lady from Westphalia had put the victorious 'weapon' in our hands – a pair of slippers, which she had sent in the Christmas parcel to one of the guards to the left of us, whatever use he could have made of them out here. He let the Bolsheviks hear what a nice Christmas gift he had received. Astonishment on the other side and then the question:

"What are slippers?"

A comrade who understood a little bit more of the Russian language than the rest of us, explained to Ivan what they are.

"Tufli, tufli," he shouted in 'fluent' Russian, in a class of its own, and added a description.

But the Red Army soldiers were still as struck with wonder as before. They had never seen any 'tufli.' Poor devils! They would neither have the money, nor the chance, to get a pair of slippers in the Soviet 'paradise' of workers and farmers, even if they ever came home from the war at all, and still had their feet!

The triumph was complete. You could almost talk about total destruction, because over there they seemed absolutely struck dumb. Imagine how warm inside that old woman over there in Westphalia would be as she, in the next field-post letter, read what a great moral victory she had helped us to win.

They were bad losers, those Red Army soldiers. They completely lost their fighting spirit and then they began to get indecent and insolent. They asked for addresses of girls in Berlin, who they said they would soon visit, and promised us a fairly acceptable existence in Siberia. The machine-gunner in our trench found it to be the last straw, as one of them said:

"Hitler soon kaput!"

"Hey, send a New Year's card to that bandit from Georgia, in the Kremlin, and tell him from us that we soon will come eastwards with our King Tigers again, and then he'll shut up for a while," he answered, shouting.

That 'dig' about King Tigers, the new 69-ton heavy tanks, that neither Russian, British nor American weapons could hurt, seemed to have an effect, because the Bolsheviks went 'soft' again. They suggested swapping Christmas gifts. They seemed especially eager to swap tobacco and cigarettes. But their *mahorka,* some sort of pipe-tobacco, a terrible brown stuff that you perhaps took when you had no moss, and that we already had come to know, with disgust, in Russia … we didn't want that!

"Very good *papirossij,* fine brand Aviatik ," said one of the voices appealingly, from the other side of the railway embankment. Aviatik is one of the better cigarette brands among the Russians.

"All right! You get a packet of fine German tobacco for four packets of Aviatik," said one of our comrades, who already had vainly tried to swap a packet of tobacco, dry as dust, among us in the company. The tobacco, under all circumstances, was better than the Russian *mahorka,* so he was not unfair to the Bolshevik.

They both climbed out of their trenches and approached each other. It was a strange meeting between east and west. The tall SS-man was in a white snow-suit, with his assured, half nonchalant and death-defying bearing – *morituri te salutant.* The stocky Red Army soldier, like an Eskimo, was in a quilted uniform with a rolling, splashing walk. Just as they were within reach of each other, a bullet whistled past from a guard further away, who did not know the situation, and had seen the two figures. They ran away from each other with giant leaps and disappeared under cover, as flashes came from different directions.

"Now you've pissed in your trousers!" someone shouted at the hastily returned exchanger who, annoyed and embarrassed after the first fright, only muttered something incomprehensible and undoubtedly very indecorous.

While we had been associating in this 'civil' way with the deadly enemy, the Division's staff had received reports about the events occurring here. Suspecting mischief, the Divisional commander had given orders to aim all available weapons at the terrain in front of our sector, ready to fire if something should happen. But all remained peaceful. Gradually it went silent. Soon dawn would come and then it would be time for the Bolsheviks to move back, if they wanted to avoid getting shovelled into the hard frozen ground of Courland as corpses.

# 2

# Courland Finale

For a few more days our company stayed in the desolate mound of stones at Bunkas, that fly-speck on the map. Nothing much happened during that time. The machine-gun position that Ivan had managed to place so troublesomely for the company commander's bunker the day before New Year's Eve, had been turned into nothing but a memory on New Years day by our mortars.

On 2 January orders came from the Division's staff that we should take prisoners in our sector of the division. A complete Russian army had vanished into thin air from a sector further south, and as headquarters expected a major Russian attack against us in the near future they thought that the missing army was lying in front of us. They wanted to get a clear idea of the situation.

A reconnaissance party consisting of eight men from our company went out. Their target was a Russian machine-gun position by a group of trees, about 100 metres in front of our lines. Before that my eight good 8cm mortars began to isolate the target, at its rear and to its flanks. As heavy infantry guns joined in, the Russian MG team over there became practically cut off from their own men. At dawn the snow-suited 'recce' party went out.

While the mortars and guns pinned down the Red Army soldiers, our patrol quickly worked their way forward. Everything worked all right until the 'rush-in.' Then, as the men ran the last metres to overpower the Russians, it became clear that the ground had been mined. One after the other they went into the air. The Russians were warned and ran for their lives. One of our soldiers managed to grab a running Russian by the foot, but at the same time stepped on a mine. One man fell and the remaining seven returned, unsuccessful and more or less badly wounded.

During the night our neighbouring company got the chance to complete the same task. Their patrol was luckier and actually captured a Russian. But, on the way back to our lines, the prisoner managed to pick up a knife when unguarded for a moment, and cut his own throat. He died without a sound. The two SS men with him were completely covered in blood.

Two days later we were relieved and could leave Bunkas, a real death trap. It lay in the open without any connections to the rear, except during the dark of the night. We were lucky to get out of there before Ivan had finished with the build-up for the great assault in this sector that we knew would come. Instead, our successors had to face the storm a few days later and according to what I later heard, hardly anyone from the relief came out of there alive.

5 January was a day of rest. No guard duty in rock-hard, frozen trenches and foxholes, where you could feel the cold come creeping, centimetre by centimetre, up your legs. No bombardment, no insidious snipers, no sudden diving fighter-planes. Once again you could wash properly, shave, and stretch out in peace and quiet, with a cigarette between clean fingers. The pressing and wearying insecurity of the front had gone. It felt wonderful to get a chance to take off our 'lousy' uniforms and let our skin enjoy clean underwear. We undertook some weapon cleaning and then went off to the front-line cinema. We could only hear the noise from the front as an indistinct mumble. During the afternoon the Russian artillery, with all barrels 'playing', performed a menacing overture to the coming assault.

In the nicely heated cinema parlour the white screen showed scenes from other fronts in the latest newsreels. There we saw smartly-dressed, clean and well-fed people in comfortable apartments, with carpets, armchairs and shining lamps, books and music. They had well-cooked food on fine china, with silver cutlery and white tablecloths. It was like a dream to us front-line soldiers. Month after month we had lain outdoors in mud and slush, ice and snow, with death as our closest comrade, and all the time had only seen other men in field-grey. Bearded, dirty and worn out, we were driven to breaking point by the fighting.

After having slept all night, undisturbed by the noise of fighting and assaults, the company went to the front for a new task the following day. The short rest had restored us, and after arrival at the new combat-sector at Priekule, about 40 kilometres east of the port-town of Libau, we began to establish ourselves as well as we could. A position for my platoon was pointed out to me, behind a hill. As well as our 8cm mortars, we had about 30 *Stuka zu Fuß*, the soldiers' name for a new rocket weapon of a mortar type, mounted on a simple wooden frame, with a projectile-weight of 82 kilos and 28cm calibre, electrically fired.

For the first few days all was peaceful in Priekule, but one morning all hell broke loose. With sudden violence Stalin organs began their unmerciful hammering. It went on for days, except for short pauses, as the Russian infantry attempted to break through our sector. Our mortar position was one of the first targets of the fire storm. Closer and closer, with only a few metres interval, the projectiles of the Stalin organs fell thick and fast. As the artillery began to participate in the bombardment, it became almost unbearable to lie pressed down in an uncertain wait. The ground around us trembled, the logs in the earthen bunker wailed and moaned under the hits, and frozen mud strained down through the chinks.

The fire storm rose towards afternoon to the wildest fury, now obviously with the company to our left as the most important target. During this violent bombardment orders were received that our mortars should go into action. The only thing to do was to take a deep breath and run out into that hell. The area around us had completely changed character. The small differences of level that were there before the shelling had been ploughed away by Ivan's artillery and a new landscape created. The shell craters lay as close as the holes in a Swiss cheese. One of the mortars had obviously taken a direct hit down the barrel, because the remains hung like an opened banana-skin over the mounting. The other mortars had survived, as had the stock of shells, about 150 of them. They were lying there ready to be sent over to Ivan with a grim greeting.

What then followed was, for me, one of the most frantic moments of the war. I guess it would have been too much to hope that the enemy should cease firing at our mortar position, so that we, in peace and quiet, could carry out our own attack! However, their fire did not show any sign of slackening at all. Every other minute you had to throw yourself down some hole to avoid being torn to pieces by a howling shell. During this we had to maintain firing, according to the corrections that the field-telephone blared to us direct from the artillery observer, who was somewhere out there in front of us. I myself ran, with a car-battery in my arms, from one *Stuka zu Fuß* to the next (they were fired electrically) together with Erich Lindenau. After each firing we ran for the nearest crater, then up with the battery, like a babe in arms, and away with the next shell.

In that way we kept going all afternoon, hour after hour. The stock of ammunition ran out, but new boxes were delivered without any interruption in our firing. With wet blankets we ran from mortar to mortar, to cool off the gleaming hot barrels. Our rounds spread a terrible destruction among the charging Russian infantry waves. Exactly on the metre the shells hit their designated targets, which was as a result of the first day's careful correctional firing.

For ten days and nights this slaughter at Priekule went on. Only at dawn, or sometimes in the afternoon, was there a pause, as the yellow-brown Russian infantry soldiers started to crawl out of their hideouts and spread over the terrain in front of our lines. Then a silence from the heavier weapons on the other side occurred with an almost violent abruptness. But the silence was of very short duration, because the next moment the first shouts of *urrää* from the storming Bolsheviks were drowned by the murderous defensive fire from our mortars, from the fast-firing MG 42, and from the submachine-guns closest to the enemy. Wave after wave of attackers poured forth, but they were all crushed to pieces, or fell back and faded. Our line held!

In the last few days we had observed how political commissars – *politruki* - followed behind the infantry assaults. After several days of vain attacks, and with heavy losses, the Russians panicked as they came out into the open terrain. As soon as they showed any sign of panic or escape, the commissars shot their own troops, without mercy.

About 20 January our Division was pulled out of the inferno at Priekule. It was the former commander of the 'Wiking' Division, *SS-Obergruppenführer* Steiner, at that time commander of III (Germanic) SS *Panzerkorps*, who now sent us, via Libau, over the Baltic Sea to Stettin. Whether he transferred us out of fondness for his old hardened division, or for strictly military reasons, may be left unsaid, but that transfer saved many lives in Division 'Nordland'.

Stettin, on 22 January, was a sad sight. The inner city had been more or less blown away, or burned down, by British and American bombers. Piles of broken household goods, bricks and rubble framed the streets in front of the facades of blackened houses. Between them moved pale, dead-tired and after five years of clothes rationing, threadbare people who, with resolute defiance and fighting-spirit, still went about their daily occupations.

We drove directly through the town, without stopping. The march proceeded north-east and our destination was Freiheide, a small place 8 kilometres north of the town of Massow, in Pomerania, the centre of a blooming peasant district. There we had almost two, wonderful, peaceful weeks. Mornings and afternoons were, of course, filled with exercises in close combat, and weapons training. This was necessary even when the frontline soldier had come to rest far behind the line.

However, in the evenings we were free, and were welcomed with open arms by the local inhabitants. The farmers, most of them of the generation that was out at the Front in the First World War, did not know how they could make our stay there pleasant enough. Almost every evening there was dancing in the barn, in one of the magnificent and well-managed farms, to the music of a local musician or some soldiers playing the accordion. SS men danced with the farmers' daughters, who were healthy and well-fed young women.

If there was no dancing in the evening our company commander would invite the inhabitants to a 'comrades' evening in the camp. It is true that we had no sensational attractions to show, as when we still had 'old' Ragnar Johansson among us. He was an extremely strong Swede, in front of whom the whole company had shivered. Under the influence of strong fluids and with a wild look in his eyes, he would look for *Mussulmen*, as he called the ethnic Germans from Rumania and whom, even in a sober state, he found it hard to accept. It was unlikely that there was a stronger man in the Division. He used to perform at our comrades' evenings by bending horseshoes, hitting nails through oak planks with his bare hands, and having a couple of men strike with sledgehammers a large stone that had been laid upon his broad chest. On one occasion, he ran two kilometres in combat, with a large shell-splinter sticking out of his back, being chased by Russians, and with the naked, muscular upper part of his body covered with blood.

In between times we got to know the fine, old, peasant culture of this countryside, so closely related to that of our Swedish peasants. Certainly our world, the front-line soldiers' world, was quite different from theirs. Although hardened front-line soldiers, with our whole way of life concentrated in the present, we felt a deep respect for their many centuries-old, family traditions. We respected their quiet, strong way of walking their own path through life. Their world of ideas and religious thinking had its roots in time immemorial, which found expression in embroideries, textiles, furniture and household utensils of Nordic style and beauty of form.

While we were lying in this stillness in the rich peasant district of Pomerania, the war out there grew to a hell without limit. The German offensive in the Ardennes, that in the beginning seemed so promising, came to a standstill, and was followed by superior pressure from the Anglo-American armies. At the same time, the 'Red surge' broke through and crossed the Vistula, in which the German people had put their trust. Suddenly we were in the combat zone again.

# 3

# Massow

In the second week of February we were once again face to face with the Bolsheviks. Since the Vistula position had been broken through, the situation at the front had changed radically. A great proportion of the heavy equipment and weapons had been lost, for instance much artillery. At the same time it had become more difficult to get replacements from Germany, as the never-ending bombings put the traffic into chaos. The Red Army could throw forward brand new corps of artillery, and immense numbers of tanks, without interruption. Especially effective was the new Stalin tank with its enormous 122mm calibre gun.

I remember one specific situation as we fired off a battery of 10.5cm infantry guns as fire support, when with the naked eye I could see more than 200 gun-barrels on the other side. The Bolsheviks had not even bothered to camouflage them, since our air force was involved with the bombers over western Germany. This superior power in artillery, aircraft and tanks, which was almost always followed by a never-ending swarm of infantry, a Red Army mix of Russians, Kalmuks, Kirghizians, Turkomens, etc, we met with *Panzerfäuste*, mortars, machine-guns and submachine-guns, and perhaps an assault gun or a King Tiger. It was like facing an automatic weapons assault with a stone and a sling, but we held out!

… It was just east of Massow. The main frontline followed the edge of a forest. I was ordered to take up a forward position with seven men. From a slight depression in the field we were to stop Russian infantry attacks with two machine guns, model MG 42. We had arrived at night in our section to take over from a *Wehrmacht* unit. Barely arrived, I had to go forward with my men and our MGs. In pouring rain and pitch black darkness we groped our way to our three pits. I took the middle one with Gebauer, a German farmer's son from Rumania, and brought the MG in position, hoping that we would have some cover when day broke. The second MG was to our left with three boys and the remaining three crawled into the pit to the right with assault rifles and MPi's (the German version of 'tommy guns').

In case of an attack this position was hopeless! There was no connecting trench back to the main line. Only at night could one crawl back to 'safety'. We could only hope that the Reds would keep quiet. They did, but only 'til early morning. First came an overture by the Russian artillery. As they kept up their fire for hours, with increasing intensity, we little mice hiding in our holes began to understand that this was not any little artillery softening up. The avalanche of shrapnel raged back and forth over our whole sector as far as we could hear and guess. Mercilessly it ploughed the field from one end to the other. As darkness again fell, the fire from the muzzles lit up the horrible landscape almost like searchlights in an air attack on a city. We huddled as best we could to survive this ordeal. The weather changed and the rain turned into a drizzle but steady and grey in small droplets, gradually becoming hazy. The muddy soil in and around our pits dissolved into a porridge-like muddle that oozed up over our boots, smearing our weapons and making us miserable. Within a couple of hours our uniforms were soaked. The coat, heavy even under normal conditions, had absorbed so much water that it felt heavy as lead. The mud in our boots made a sucking noise. Luckily most of the fire went over our heads, because the men before us had made a good job of hiding our position. Only occasional shells burst in our immediate vicinity. The main line behind us bore the brunt of the hail of steel and fire.

For three days and three nights we had to lie in these godforsaken pits, waiting, waiting, waiting … The rain started pouring again. No food reached us, any connection backwards was unthinkable as long as the fire raged between us and the company. In the morning twilight of the fourth day Gebauer had the watch. The rest of us were lying half asleep and starved in the mud totally exhausted. Suddenly Gebauer shook me violently: "They are coming!"

A quick glance through the camouflage. There, only thirty metres away, a drove of Bolsheviks were approaching - no time to panic! They were well on the way to try to overrun our company. It seems that they had not yet discovered our well-hidden position. In spite of the foggy air I could already see a second wave of infantry emerging from the haze, only fifty metres behind the first one. I got the machine gun going and fired for all I was worth. My fire and the screams of the wounded woke up the other boys, and our weapons spat fire and death on the brown masses.

The wild firing soon got a reaction from the surviving attackers, who had gone to ground and discovered us. I happened to look to the left and saw a Bolshevik working his way through a depression towards us, to get at us from behind. In the same instant he saw me and disappeared. There he was again! He aimed a burst from his sub-machine gun at me. The lead whistled around my ears. The duel was on! The distance was hardly twenty metres. I got hold of an assault rifle and waited for him. Gebauer had to handle the MG alone. We took turns shooting at each other - head up, head down, up, down. Martin, the *Rottenführer* with the other MG in my group, could have touched the Russian if he had looked in that direction but he did not notice our duel. Finally the Russian made a mistake. Either because he was too lazy or in order to fire more quickly, he let his machine-gun stay up, visible to me, while he ducked down to wait for my next shot. I squeezed the trigger then stayed up with my finger on the trigger. There! His head was up again behind his weapon, and before he could react he had a hole between the eyes. The head was thrown back, then sank, disappeared and his limp hand dropped his weapon.

Furious, the Bolsheviks threw themselves against this unexpected little obstacle that our position became. The situation was hopeless but the boys fought formidably. The circle around us became ever tighter. In the heat of the battle one of the boys in the pit to the right straightened up with his machine-pistol and let it make a sweep that killed maybe ten of the enemy, giving us some breathing space, but he soon sank down, shot through the belly. There was less pressure but we had lost one of our brave men. We would not be able to hold much longer, but the enemy lay in lifeless heaps around our position. I sent up a red signal rocket: "Enemy attacking!" No sign of life behind us. Maybe they had got so used to the artillery fire that had rushed over our heads that they were now asleep, while we up front were fighting for our lives? Another red rocket. No reaction. I got boiling mad at our men back there and could have cried with fury. While I helped Gebauer to feed the machine gun with new ammunition I could hear myself swearing non stop, wishing them the worst possible tortures in hell

I let Gebauer handle the machine gun alone while I fired alternatively with the assault rifle and with my machine-pistol. He forgot the danger, pushing his chest above the parapet in order to fire better. "Down!" I screamed through the hellish noise. He reacted with a reckless laugh, just nineteen years old … and continue to send a devastating fire into the attackers.

Another Red Army wave came rolling forward to smash us. They were totally unprotected in the open field. Gebauer lifted his head to see better. "Head down!" I screamed. Too late! Gebauer suddenly jerked backwards and sank to one side. I turned him around towards me. He was hit under the left eye, the bullet passing through his neck. He was still alive, blood flowing down from cheek and neck. He embraced me, his fading eyes looking at me desperately. He begged, "Write to my mother ..." His embrace slackened, the arms sank while he whispered, "Just a few lines ..." And then I was alone, so alone and miserably small in my fox-hole. Something like panic tried to get hold of me. I made an effort to think, "Calm, just calm, take it easy ...", but my whole body was shaking.

Martin was now also alone. I called out to him to take his weapon and come over. He came rushing with wild leaps. To the right also one boy was left. All the others had died with a bullet through their head. We got him over to us. I implored them to try and keep their heads down. Of course, Martin in his eagerness forgot my advice. That was enough and he broke down seconds later with a bullet just above the nose ridge. With our machine guns (the MG42 was unsurpassed, the fastest of its kind in the whole war) we two survivors managed to keep the enemy down and away. For some inexplicable reason we didn't receive any incoming mortar or artillery fire. Maybe the fighting units were too mixed, too confused. Suddenly we heard from behind the roars of "urraaa". They had broken through!

"Grab the gun and run!" I bellowed to my comrade, as I got hold of my own MG, hooked some ammunition belts around my neck, and carrying an ammunition box was soon out of my position. Zig-zagging over the field in a crazy run, we reached what was left of the 'protective' edge of the wood. My comrade was a few leaps behind me. As I threw a quick glance behind me, I saw him grab his chest, then fall forward. From the cover of the trees, I looked up once more and saw him lying there, weakly waving at me. Too late, nothing doing - the Russians were already there! I kept running and reached a glade among the trees. Four Bolsheviks come rushing from one side with their tommy guns spitting lead at me. I dropped my gun, all the ammunition, and flew more than ran, with the bullets whistling around me and ploughing into the ground around my legs. Theoretically I was already a dead *Unterscharführer*, but a soldier must have luck! That is what I had that day. I dived in among the trees further on, and all of a sudden I found myself in the midst of our company - now numbering only a handful ... there was our Swedish commander smoking a cigarette. He looked me up and down and said, "It's not that bad! Could be worse." With his calmness I felt embarrassed, standing in front of him short of breath (my chest could have burst!) - shaking and sweating after the tremendous tension. (Much later I found out that his calmness was a fake to avoid panic amongst the few men he still had in his company. In the course of a few hours it had lost more than half its strength. In the midst of this cauldron of death, screams, groans, and mutilated, blooded bodies, his pretended nonchalance and complete calmness saved the lives of our surviving men. Such an officer one could follow all the way to hell and back!)

The company commander sent out a couple of men to re-establish the connection with the neighbouring units. One man was sent back with a report on the dangerous situation. An *Oberscharführer* received the order to make a counter-attack with three men. I was one of those so 'privileged'. Some counter-attack! Four men against an enemy force of probably more than a company's size! And these four totally exhausted, physically and mentally gone following the last four hours of shocking happenings. It did not make sense, this promise of certain death, but discipline and the feeling of duty urged us on.

Death surrounded us from all sides, pushing us on and seeming to give us wings. With wild roars of "Hurrah" we push on through thickets and bushes and fired madly against the swarm of brown figures rising everywhere and turning to flee our impetuous attack. Suddenly, a Bolshevik stood before me, barely three or four metres away, his face a rigid scared stare. My short burst of bullets before he had time to squeeze the trigger made him keel over with a harsh groan as I rushed past him. We recaptured the whole wooded sector in a matter of minutes that to us seemed an eternity, encompassing our whole lives. We reached the edge and threw ourselves into the previous position of the company and continued firing furiously at the stream of enemy infantry now fleeing from the wood towards a low ridge beyond the field that offered them protection. Two stragglers jumped blindly over us and dropped just a few steps beyond our trench with perforated backs. The whole field was covered with fallen enemy soldiers. And all four of us alive! Incredible, inconceivable! We looked at each other, radiant in this bloody mess and mass of death – we could have cheered. What a counter-attack! But my heart thundered ready to burst. We were totally exhausted, and a reaction of fatigue set in.

By and by the rest of the company drifted back to the recovered positions. My commander ordered me back to the death trap of my fox-hole, where I had already lost seven boys. All alone with my MG, surrounded by fallen SS men and enemies! Never before had I felt so miserable , forlorn. I would rather have thrown away my MG and run far, far away, but there it was again, that damned feeling of duty. It held me in a steely grip.

I become aware of a steady groan nearby. Peering cautiously I saw that it was one of our boys. He had a bullet through both hips and the underbelly. I made him roll over on my back, then crawled slowly towards our defensive line with this heavy burden. The risk of being seen by the Russians was better not thought of, but we made it! The same *Oberscharführer* who led our 'counter-attack' saw us and came crawling to help me. Once in safety we get hold of a stretcher and carried him to the rear. Here we found a big barn, where the floor was covered with dead, dying, and seriously wounded, some of them our close comrades. We hurried out of this place of groans, screams and death rattles - back again to my lonely foxhole! I noticed in the two o'clock direction some vague movements in the vegetation. A glance through my binoculars - Russians! A quick report to my commander. Already as I glided down into my MG pit, the first 10.5 cm shells came whooshing over my head, ploughing through the terrain and smashing a Red Army attack before it could get going.

Twilight sank over the torn battlefield. Soon it was completely dark. It became cold and my teeth chattered as I sat there behind my weapon in the scary darkness. Pictures passed through my feverish head, grotesque pictures of wounded comrades and the slowly fading eyes of the dying Gebauer. Now and then I got a fright hearing the faint noises of some Soviet night patrol. All night they came, testing and prying, their wheezing whispers so near.

Towards dawn relief came. A company from a *Wehrmacht* division took over the defence of our section. We returned to our vehicles for a journey to a few days of rest – the pitiful remnant of what just a few days before had been a fully equipped company of SS *Panzergrenadiers.*

For a full week after the Massow affair my hands shook so intensely that I could hardly light a cigarette. And the company that had relieved us? Just a few days later there were no survivors!

For a few lovely days we could rest from the struggle, check our equipment, including the half-tracks and the weapons, and write letters. The spring had come early to this fertile part of Pomerania. The sun shone strongly from a clear blue sky every day. The lush green grass was already sprouting up from the fertile soil. Here and there grew colourful patches of anemones and other spring flowers, and the swallows flew up and away with 'spring-dizzy' warbles. It was wonderful to lie on your back in the fresh grass, with closed eyes in the sunshine, and think of anything but the war. The warmth had long ago melted the ice on the ponds and small lakes, and we could already, at the end of February, take a daily bath in a small lake near the property where we were stationed. Our scarred and exhausted bodies became strong and vigorous again.

But the wave from the east rose and rose, and came implacably closer. It was thrown forward on tens of thousands of American trucks, and was fed by many millions of tons of American supplies. It had already crushed the outer bastions of western civilisation against the east, and its cultural monuments. The fruits of Nordic-Germanic colonisers, after thousands of years of hard work, and after steadfast struggle against the barbaric, ravaging expeditions of the Asian hordes, had now been destroyed.

But still we believed! Should our part of the world be ruined because a few, temporarily powerful, were blinded? In their hatred, and with all their power, they had helped to break down the barrier beneath a torrent of barbarism and brutal rawness, that in wild anger threw itself against our protective wall. We had seen too many examples of youthful bravery, enthusiasm and spirit of self-sacrifice in our lines, as self-appointed defenders of the west, to believe in the dreadful prophesies of Oswald Spengler: "the demise of the Occident".

The only thing that disturbed our equanimity during the wonderful days of rest and peace were American and Russian fighter-planes that sometimes came diving from the sky, and with their guns turned road users into bloody shreds. These attacks were not just against us soldiers, but also against the farmers in the fields, their wives and daughters, and against the small children on their way to school. This made us furious.

Soon rumbling could be heard to the east. The thunder came quickly closer. But there was no need to march to the front. It came to us! The local inhabitants began to pack their most important and precious belongings on wheelbarrows and carts, to try to escape this new Mongol storm, the women weeping and wringing their hands, the old steady farmers with a hard demeanour and fiercely compressed lips.

Towards evening the transports with wounded began to pass us. We had become used to going down to the road in the evenings, to smoke a last cigarette before the tattoo, and to chat with the locals and perhaps meet a girl. But that evening we stayed in the camp. None of us wanted to see the wounded and mutilated, with their blood-soaked bandages, uniforms torn to pieces, and pain-filled faces. Why be reminded of a fate that, in a few hours, could strike each and every one of us?

The state of agitation in facing the unknown, over there at the front, rose every hour. When we were actually lying there, in the front-line, it was not too bad. Then, the hectic tension and the permanent mortal danger kept such thoughts away. The worst were those hours of agonised waiting before the action.

The distant thunder continued during the night. I would lie awake until dawn, listening. I was not the only one to be sleepless. We lay smoking, talking in whispers about anything and everything, trying to think about other things than what was waiting for us. Others, who had gone to sleep, were haunted by terrible nightmares, and tossed and turned in the hay.

# 4

# Vossberg

In the morning the platoons were reported as 'ready to march,' to the company commander. A short briefing about the situation and then we marched off. Out on the main road we met the first fleeing civilians, who came with their household goods on handcarts and horse-drawn carts. They looked as if they had been on the road all night. Their clothes were covered with yellow-grey dust and they looked at us with sad eyes that were red with weariness. But still they waved to us, as we passed in our half-tracks. The march continued slowly, because the number of refugees increased along the road.

After a few kilometres we ran into a medical convoy from the *Wehrmacht,* taking care of about one hundred miserable old men, women and small children. Some American fighter-planes had created this massacre just a little while previously. In the ditch beside an ambulance, a young woman sat with a bloody bundle in her arms. The blood streamed down the left side of her face, from a flap of her forehead that hung down over her eyes. She rocked the lifeless shred in her arms, with a continual monotonous groan, crying, "My baby, my baby!"

The column halted. Three dead horses, with overturned carriages, had to be moved from the road before we could go on. The groaning of the wounded and mutilated refugees grated upon our ears. We became furious when we saw the result of these cruel ravages among the defenceless.

The march had to go on. We continued in silence. The terrible sights had made us lose the mood for chatting and joking with the kind of black humour that we always used just before combat. The column turned north-east, obviously length-wise to the front-line as the battle-sounds did not come closer. The whole *Aufklärungs Abteilung* was gathered. In long columns, on parallel running roads, we rolled forward with great distances and gaps. No bombers or fighter-planes disturbed us. There was a short halt and then the march continued. It was getting towards evening. Obviously there would be no action for us that day.

The column rolled on through the flat Pomeranian countryside, past well-kept farms, and magnificent country houses with many hundreds of years of old traditions. We continued, beyond rows of trees that grew

31

straight as arrows, and past small stone churches. Would all this, in a few days, lie in ruins under heavy clouds of battle smoke? It was getting dark, and turned to night, but we kept moving on. To the right the horizon was lit up by a fluttering red light. It was the front-line, with all its noises. There were burning houses against a black sky, roaring attacks and counter-attacks, one moment silence, the next a painful death. The thunder of artillery slowly died down, but we were now so close that we could hear the distant firing from automatic weapons.

Towards the early morning of 3 March, we reached the large village of Vossberg. A longer halt was ordered while the company commanders went to the *Abteilung* commander for a briefing, and received their orders. All seemed quiet and peaceful in the village and its neighbourhood. Certainly rifle and machine-gun fire was heard irregularly some kilometres away, but not so that it bothered us.

It was nice to get a chance to leave the half-tracks and stretch out. The inhabitants had already left the village. Together with *Oberscharführer* Kunze I entered a grand house. We found a bedroom immediately behind the big kitchen. In the beds only the mattresses were left, but on the other hand what should we do with white sheets and eiderdowns? It was nice to take a nap. We decided that we had better keep our boots on. You never knew what would happen … Sleep came quickly. I hardly heard Kunze's first wild snores before I too was asleep.

A terrible boom suddenly brought us up from a deep sleep. Like a shot I was out of the bed and into the kitchen, with Kunze right behind. Brraaammmm! Our eardrums fluttered from the 'boom', in the room we had just left. We could not resist taking a look back in there, before we rushed out of the house. Where Kunze had been lying a few seconds before, lounging at full length, the remains of a mattress and bed lay, in a huge mess, on the floor among shell splinters and mortar fragments. Kunze grinned at me with a roar of laughter, "Lucky again, eh!"

Yes! That was the kind of luck the front-line soldier must have. A soldier without it would never get the time to become a hardened front-line soldier, before his career would be over. Crouched down, we ran out into the village street. There, everyone was running around trying to get into the vehicles. Towards me came Erich Lindenau from my platoon. He was running, and excited in a way very uncommon for this veteran, who was always cool as a cucumber. "We are trapped! T-34s are coming from the western entrance!" he shouted.

Once again, the dull 'barks' from the tank guns could be heard. We crouched down, waiting for the impact of the shells, ready to throw ourselves down flat on the street. The shots were too high. In all the chaos, infantry soldiers from the Wehrmacht came in from the east. Panting, they told us that Russian infantry were attacking from that direction. What a hell of a mess! Russian tanks were preventing one way out, our way of retreat, and Russian infantry were blocking the other!

The second platoon dashed off, running among the burning houses, to stop the infantry. At the same time a huge colossus came rolling up the village main street. A King Tiger, it filled the width of the street. The commander, a young *Unterscharführer*, was half running in front of the tank, guiding the driver with hand signals. It bumped into one of the houses and crushed half the gable, then clattered on and drove up into the middle of the square. What passion for combat you get, when such a giant comes to your aid!

In a gap between two houses I could see the Russian tanks down on the highway. It was a long, curved avenue and they could be dimly seen through the trees. There were eight or ten T-34s. They were firing non-stop at the fully visible King Tiger. Their shells bounced off, like peas, from its powerful armour. Completely unconcerned, the crew aimed their gun. The enthusiasm of our men over this supreme invulnerability had no limit. The muzzle-flashes shot in a constant stream out of the long barrel. Already the flames were licking the hull of the nearest T-34 and in no time four of them were put out of action. Four T-34s in four minutes! The remaining tanks tried to quickly retreat, but were shot to pieces. We cheered the King Tiger whose gunner emerged, showing a happy, grinning, sooty face from out of the turret's hatch.

"Out of the village!" came the order.

Then the Russian artillery started hammering too, and we rushed to the half-tracks. The commander's armoured car from another company drove first, and after it mine followed at 50 metres distance. Full throttle! At full tilt the column dashed out of the dangerous 'nest,' past the smoking, knocked-out Russian tanks, whose crews lay dead around them.

We drove parallel to a highway under construction, which a few hundred metres further away ran across our road on a viaduct. In a gap I could see the men from the 2nd platoon come running over the field to meet us beyond the viaduct. Just as we came down into the bend, the car in front of us slipped sideways in the gravel and had an engine failure, right under the viaduct. Only an inch behind, my driver managed to stop our half-track and the whole column stopped, tightly packed together. What damned bad luck!

But that was not all! About 150 metres away from us, three Russian anti-tank guns had taken position beyond the viaduct, and started shooting at us through the tunnel. With smoke-grenades we tried to make ourselves as invisible as possible. I chased out the whole crew. The driver, once out of the vehicle, grabbed the machine-gun from the rack on the half-track. I threw myself into the ditch, to keep the Russians pinned down with my fire. Their shells landed horribly close. Some were a few metres behind, some a few metres ahead, and I was just waiting for the direct hit as I saw their muzzle-flashes.

Someone was hit by splinters and cried out. Comrades came running and lifted him into the vehicle. All the time others were working hard to get the vehicle started, out there in front of us. Finally! All the men were aboard except myself. Up with the machine-gun, into the half-track that was already travelling at high speed. I jumped up on the front. In normal circumstances I would not had been able to make that jump! Friendly hands pulled me to safety. Under our fierce fire with three guns, the Russians, in this wild rain of fire, did not think of shooting, and our column dashed through the tunnel and away from the danger zone.

As we followed a bend in the road, a few kilometres further away there lay a small village. About 100 metres in front of us, a group of Bolsheviks stood there at the roadside, occupied with unhitching a small horse-drawn cart that pulled an anti-tank gun. As they saw that it was German vehicles that came towards them, they ran panicking in all directions. The small commander's car avoided the horse-cart, but I let my half-track drive straight at it. Some Russians who had not got out of the way, stood there, stiff with fear. With a crash the cart was splintered. A soft body bounced against the armour of our vehicle, and the column dashed on, while the machine-guns caught the fleeing soldiers in short bursts, cutting them down.

The Bolsheviks seemed to be everywhere. They must have made a real breakthrough. Just beyond the village stood *Untersturmführer* Schwarz from the 4th Company. How he got there was a mystery. He gave the signal to halt. I reported, but he just waved impatiently with his hand.

"You, drive your vehicle into cover down there in the depression and take up position 100 metres out in the field!"

"*Untersturmführer*! I have orders not to leave my half-track, " I protested, "even if your situation is desperate." I could see that he was under stress.

"I will report you for refusing orders!" he shouted.

The two closest following half-tracks had made a smart turn by our side. The crews jumped out and gathered by the vehicle furthest away. Crack! A shell landed in the middle of the group! Right in front of our eyes they were all torn to pieces. The road was under Russian artillery fire! *Untersturmführer* Schwarz changed his mind, jumped into one of the crewless half-tracks and bawled "Drive like hell!"

Two kilometres further ahead, a small group of SS men stood staring at a bloody bundle at the roadside. As we slowed, I looked down, to see a waving hand rise up from all the blood. The vehicle stopped and I heard an indistinct voice call my name. Oh, God! It was my fellow countryman *Untersturmführer* Meyer, the favourite of the company!

He was almost unrecognisable. A splinter had cut his chin in two and stuck in a neck vertebra. He was a few millimetres from death! He had also been shot in the shoulder, and his chest was covered with blood. His legs were pierced by an immense number of shrapnel fragments. But he was alive, and even tried to tell me of his misadventure. But his voice was weak. With his damaged chin his speech was slurred, and only about half of what he said was comprehensible.

"We'll take you to the nearest first-aid station," I told him.

It was remarkable how lucky, at the same time as having such bad luck, this magnificent boy had been. He had already been reported as 'fallen in combat' once before. It was in Estonia when, badly wounded, he had been taken care of by another unit and been laid among several other dead and badly wounded in a barn. It was a provisional first-aid station. By mistake his combat tunic, with pay-book and other identity-papers, was switched with those of a soldier already dead, and he was reported to the company commander as dead.

It had been hard having to lose our cheerful comrade, who steadfastly drank his milk and, despite all seductive tricks, refused to drink his ration of alcohol, which he instead generously passed on to more thirsty souls in the company. We had mourned him sincerely for a long time. Not so much for the liquor, even though perhaps one or another at certain times gave Meyer's rations a sad thought, but because he was one of the best. His father, a professor at Stockholm University, received a cable of condolences from our supreme commander, Heinrich Himmler. Then, one fine day, Meyer popped up again, certainly a little bit scarred, but otherwise bright and breezy. With his almost pedantic care for the military ceremonies, he gave a perfect report to the amazed company commander. Another Swedish officer in the company had written a letter of condolence to Meyer's parents, in Sweden. That officer himself was hit by splinters, which luckily meant that the letter never reached them.

With extreme care, helpful hands lifted him up into the half-track and we drove on, with our wounded in the cramped space. The other men on the road were taken into the nearest vehicles and we drove on to more peaceful areas

In the next village we met the commander of the entire *Aufklärungs Abteilung, Sturmbannführer* Saalbach, and his staff. I reported with the wounded men, who were carried out of the half-track and laid on the ground. As Saalbach stepped forward to take a look at them, Meyer made a desperate attempt to 'lie to attention,' making a faint salute with his arm and bubbling an incomprehensible report. It was easy to see that the battle-hardened commander was touched by the outstanding bearing of his youngest officer, even in such pain. But he just said, "You just look terrible."

Then the wounded were carried away. The badly wounded Meyer made it, of course. The doctors picked out all the iron 'scrap' except one small piece, which remained in his neck as a souvenir, for the rest of his life. But he never returned to the company.

# 5

# Grosswachtlin

After Vossberg we had the gaps in our ranks filled with new men from the training battalions during a lull in the fighting. They were mostly young boys from the Hitler Youth. With their burning belief and eagerness they had to be restrained so that casualties would not be unreasonably high. The 'novice' treatment that recruits usually received from hardened veterans during their first spell at the front ceased soon enough, because the boys showed that they had become fully-grown men in every respect.

Small combats and skirmishes followed, and in between we accomplished some marginally successful counter-attacks, but without making any really big gains. The front, however, had really begun to move by now. It was only the Russians' resistance to launching an attack before they had got their superior masses of artillery into position that slowed down their rate of advance. Our task seemed to be only to disturb and delay the enemy while waiting for – for what? Over and over again the Division took up position. We would make a counter-attack, withdraw to the original positions, then retreat, leaving some thinned-out company behind as the last weak barrier against one or several Russian divisions.

Amidst continuous fighting we arrived at Grosswachtlin, just east of Stettin. Some of the companies had made the usual counter-attack with considerable gain of terrain, including two important hills. Our company was then ordered forward to take over the terrain and secure the Division as it started to break free from the enemy. With my mortar platoon I was ordered to the rear, to the right of the two hills, while the other platoons would hold the nearer hill and the terrain in front of it.

We drove up with our mortar half-tracks behind the fairly protective western slope of the hill, and close below the barn next to a large farm. It was built as a square, taking up almost all the hillside. The mortars were taken from their racks on the vehicles, and brought into position in the middle of the courtyard. The correctional shootings, ordered by the company commanders who gave target instructions over the radio had to go like clockwork, as usual. There was an abundance of ammunition and we were just waiting for the Bolsheviks' attempt to attack. Then we would pepper the terrain, the depressions in the ground, and the groups of oaks at the sides where they might gather their troops for an assault.

So far they had just fired mortar shells that threw up the soil in high black fountains. Between the detonations you could hear the rattle and clatter from firearms, round the fought-over group of trees and farms out in the flat countryside. At dawn a well-known noise began. We could hear from the drone that these were Stalin tanks. Then the artillery fire was intensified. It was concentrated on a narrow area across the front, and then spread out in depth. Shouting, Red Army soldiers swarmed out of their foxholes. They ran across the fields towards our defences, newly ploughed-up by shells. It was all rattles, clatters and rumbles.

Then our moment came! The observer at the front led our mortars from point to point, with the assumed names of the fixed targets as aiming-points.

"Twenty plus on 'Erik'!" he shouted into the phone.

"Twenty plus on 'Erik'!" I repeated.

The men worked at the mortars just as we did back home on the exercise field.

"Excellent! Thirty minus on 'Manfred,' five rounds!"

The observer's voice echoed in the receiver, calm and untouched by the approaching danger. It was *Rottenführer* Kraus, one of my best men. In that way the platoon fired continuously. We changed target, aimed, fired, corrected and changed again. Round after round left the barrels with a short, dry 'bang.' Together with the small-arms of the company we forced the Bolsheviks to retreat with heavy casualties.

They could not have missed noticing the deadly activity of our mortars. It did not take long before we had their artillery fire coming at us. It whistled and howled through the air and the ground trembled. Roof trusses were splintered and flew over the courtyard. Soon the woodwork in the upper parts of the buildings, was on fire. The flames rose towards the roofs and we were surrounded by a roaring wall of fire, which reached higher and higher into the coal-black sky. The square yard was lit up as in daylight. In the glare from the fire the men looked like ghosts, as they sweated and swore while continuing to feed the red-hot barrels with rounds.

I heard no more from the observer out there in the dark. Was he dead or had the line been cut by a shell? We did not have time to find out. There was still radio contact with the company commander over the radio in my half-track. We were ordered to continue firing steadily, but with changes between the different aiming points. There was no further possibility of getting a clear view of the situation out in front.

The straw and the hay were now on fire and a heavy, humid smoke was hanging all over the farm. It was almost unendurable. The house collapsed with a dull crash. One man was wounded in the arm by a splinter, another had a piece of the calf of his leg torn away. At any moment the courtyard gate could collapse and then we would be trapped like rats. The smoke lay like a stifling and pungent lid over the farm. Our eyes were watering and it became harder to breathe.

By then we had put up with the inferno for hours, but it would not be possible for much longer. We could already hear the engines of tanks growling ever closer. They aimed their barrels at the burning farm, from the middle of which we stubbornly kept on firing rounds. The darkness began to lighten up and soon dawn would break. How should we manage to break out then? Firing from the Russians' small-arms could already be heard, threateningly close.

I ran down to the half-track to call the company commander. The line was dead! With nervous fumbling fingers I tried here and there but without any result. Without thinking of the risk of being seen against the flame-coloured background, I ran over to the north side of the hill and jumped into a bush to try to get a general view of the situation. There were muzzle-flashes from tanks only 200 metres away! I could make out the contours of the armoured giants against the lightening horizon. From the depression between the two hills I could hear Russian 'Hurrahs!' and shouts. Were we finished?

In the gateway I ran into a breathless dispatch rider from the company commander. He shouted:

"Get back! They have already broken through with their infantry!"

His face was covered with blood from a wound on the cheek and he was completely finished. We helped the many wounded into the half-tracks, and ran back to get the mortars which, in feverish haste, we mounted on the vehicles. The dispatch rider was helped up into my half-track and then we were away.

As we accelerated down the hill and out into the fields, we saw that we were surrounded by attacking Red Army soldiers. To the right, to the left and in front of us their grey-black shadows swarmed. But no-one was thinking of using the machine-guns on them, because we did not feel like announcing that they had German vehicles right in their midst. Who could tell how far away were our own soldiers?

The dispatch rider told me in a tense voice that once he discovered that the radio connection was broken the company commander had immediately sent a dispatch rider with orders to withdraw. The first one was wounded half way between the hills, but he managed to drag himself back, having been unsuccessful. At the same time as the survivors from the company got orders to mount up, the company commander had sent this second dispatch rider who only just managed to get through to us before the Bolsheviks cut the route. The 'grim reaper' had given us a few minutes' respite and we used them to forestall the total destruction of our mortar platoon. For SS men captivity meant guaranteed death by a shot in the neck, sometimes after torture.

At full throttle the half-tracks drove over the fields, reached the designated road going in the direction of Stettin-Altdamm, and some kilometres further on met the company. It had been badly knocked about. The losses had been heavy and many well-known faces could no longer be seen among the crews. The one we Swedes missed most among the fallen was Arne Johansson. He was a true Swedish socialist, who had chosen to leave his brave wife and three small children in Sweden. He wanted to protect them out here in the east, with a weapon in his hand, before the storm reached their native country. He fell, on 1 March, in a counter-attack with a handful of men, back in Ravenstein. The company commander on several occasions had to calm down his fighting spirit, which came to the fore when things started to get 'hot,' but finally it cost him his life.

# 6

# Bridgehead Stettin

The fierce Russian offensive had used large numbers of heavy artillery, and countless numbers of infantry, mainly Kirghizians, Kalmucks and other Mongolians. These nationalities became more noticeable as the Russian, Ukrainian and Siberian divisions bled to death. They implacably pressed towards our bridgehead at Stettin. The bridgehead had been reduced to the suburb of Altdamm on the eastern bank of the Oder, and its immediate neighbourhood. In the north and to the south, the Bolsheviks had already reached the bank of the Oder in these early days of March.

Stettin had to be held at all costs, so that the forces at Küstrin and Frankfurt-an-der-Oder, that were blocking the road to Berlin, could not be attacked in their flank. The Russians, as well as our senior command, had realised the vital importance of this bridgehead to the German defence. Because of that, they had sent forward everything they could manage to scrape together from other fronts. On the Courland front the fighting faded, because many of their artillery corps, armoured divisions, mortar battalions and infantry divisions, among them some of their élite troops, had been moved to the sector at Stettin-Altdamm. They were to force us back over the river.

Day and night an annihilating rain of shells of all calibres, from the heaviest howitzers, heavy Stalin organs, 120mm mortars and infantry guns, down to 37mm anti-tank-guns, beat against our positions in that narrow area. It was full of soldiers, weapons, ammunition, and supply depots. Our casualties were heavy. Pehrsson, our company commander, was wounded and brought back over the bridge to Stettin.

One of the platoon commanders in the company, *SS-Oberscharführer* Hoppe, had been blinded by an exploding bullet. He was carried down into a cellar, while two men set off to get a stretcher. A violent volley from a Stalin organ forced them back down into the cellar, where the wounded man lay on the cement floor with his face covered in blood and his eyes destroyed. Not a word did he say, but we could hear by his hard, intermittent breathing, and see by his compressed lips and hard clenched fists, that he suffered badly. As the thunder from the Stalin organ ceased, the two men said that they would go out again to try to find a stretcher. But Hoppe rose on one elbow and shouted:

"What sort of damned talk is that? An SS man walks by himself as long as he still has his legs."

Moaning, he rolled over on to his side, pushed up on his hands and rose with a great effort to his full height. In the poor daylight down there, the face of the tall *Oberscharführer* shone with a ghostly, painful whiteness behind the mask of half dried blood. With outstretched arms he stumbled, tottering for the door. Two comrades grabbed him round the waist to support him.

"Hold my arm!" he growled. "They haven't got me yet!"

We looked sadly after him, as he was taken away through the shell fire, over the small garden plots all shot to pieces, past the ruins of the small houses of the workers of Stettin, to the nearest first-aid station. His would be a difficult gap to fill. Hoppe had been a lion among SS men, strong as a bear and stubbornly death-defying. He still had his strength, but now he was as helpless as a baby, as he stumbled over shell-craters towards a life in darkness.

Under the unbroken Red assaults the bridgehead had been squeezed smaller and smaller. It now looked like a 'hedgehog-position' of the same sort that we had experienced, numerous times before, over the two years of retreat from Russia. Only one way back remained - the bridge over the Oder to Stettin. Already the frontlines ran only some 100 metres outside the city limit of Altdamm. Day and night the Russian artillery hammered on our positions and Altdamm itself, where everything lay in ruins under a dense black-brown veil of smoke over the whole area.

To get some sleep was unthinkable with the ground shaking all the time as in an earthquake, and the air thundered and vibrated with the howling and exploding shells. Pained, dirty and unshaven soldiers' faces were wherever we looked. Supplies came irregularly, although there was plenty, both in Stettin and in Altdamm. More than once the food patrols were swept away by shells on their way to the forward positions.

We could stand the hunger. Exhaustion was worse. Our eyes smarted and our faces were stiff. There was no quiet place in this burning and exploding inferno, where the groaning of the wounded filled every little pause between the shell impacts. Everywhere the shells fell with their devastating and lacerating rain of shrapnel. Walls fell down over advancing troops, or over wounded on their way to the first-aid stations. Concrete cellars tumbled inwards like boxes of toy bricks. Our underground bunkers became death traps. Rounds with delayed release from the Soviet 120mm mortars penetrated the roofs before they exploded. Trapped there, the men were struck down by the razor-sharp splinters.

With six mortars, my platoon had taken position in the yard of a house that had been completely riddled with bullets and shells. It lay a short distance outside the actual residential area of Altdamm. Among piles of broken bricks from fallen walls, twisted iron beams, radiators, and remains of furniture that had been thrown out of the windows by the explosions, the men worked with admirable calm and precision in the midst of the rain of shells. Our fire-controller, an *Unterscharführer*, was in a cellar in an advanced position. As long as the field telephone worked, the rounds rose in a continuous stream against the sky from our barrels.

No other mortar platoon could have kept up their firing, better, at least not under such conditions. But, after all, they were staunch guys, all of them. Several had been in the thick of it ever since the engagements at Narva and Dorpat. Even the newcomers stood up to prove themselves, inspired by their older comrades' calm and presence of mind. All had been hardened by the last few weeks of purgatory. They had been running the gauntlet among the Bolsheviks. After such experiences we either fell down or got stronger.

But hanging in the balance was the telephone connection. Time after time the cables were cut by shells and I had to send out two assigned signalmen to locate and repair them. Every time made my heart heavy. Hardly any soldiers had a more dangerous task than these *Strippenzieher*, and the numbers of their fallen were among the highest of all soldiers. The line breakdowns were innumerable, and then they had to go out and make repairs. I had already lost three signalmen during the few days that we had been here. They were three magnificent men. What courage, what death defiance in the rain of shrapnel!

In the evening I was ordered by the new company commander to go over myself to relieve our observer. He had had a nervous breakdown. That told me quite a lot about what was waiting for me over there. I left the command post to calm and reliable Kraus, a promising NCO, and then I was off.

The storm of artillery had decreased considerably and did not worry me too much as I went on my way. Much more violent, on the other hand, was the rattle of the infantry fire. I guessed there was close combat going on right then, somewhere over there. Explosive bullets whistled fiercely in the dark. For most of my comrades the artillery fire was the most unpleasant, but I preferred that to these damned explosive bullets, of which I was scared to death. By then they whined closer than ever around me. They hit twisted and charred branches, tree trunks, and then exploded. It was nasty, and I felt like a child afraid of ghosts when passing a dark graveyard.

It was not a long way I had to dash, just a couple of hundred metres. But it felt like an eternity. Through the dark, now and then lit up by a flare or two, or by sudden muzzle flashes, I found my way to the observation position and slid down the remains of stone stairs. As I quickly opened the door and as promptly closed it behind me, a disgusting, musty smell of old perspiration, blood and engine oil hit me.

A burning piece of cotton waste, drenched in oil in a tin can, stood beside the field radio and our observation telephone, on an elegant Chippendale table of the sort often found in northern Germany. It was the only source of light down there. It smelt and stank terribly. On a small gracefully elegant chair was an *Untersturmführer* from the staff. He was sitting there controlling the radio connections. A submachine-gun was hanging over the fine back of the chair and muddy boots scratched its fragile legs.

Moaning wheezes came from two unbelievably mutilated bodies that had been laid on the floor, with a pair of shredded and bloody overcoats as the only protection against its hard and cold cement. A medical orderly pattered to and fro between them, in hopeless attempts to ease their pain. Neither of them could live much longer. One of them had no face. Where eyes, nose, mouth and chin used to be, was only a hollowed-out, bloody mass, out of which the death wheeze pressed, squeaking and snuffling. Out of the other's left corner of the mouth ran a stream of blood. The man I had to relieve sat shrunken on the edge of a camp bed with his head buried in his hands, which nervously ploughed back and forth through his hair. At every shell's explosion that came close to us, he jumped up with fear in his eyes. In contrast to this terrible scene there sat *Untersturmführer* Schwarz, tough and unperturbed, without equal in the company.

He sat on a sugar-box beside the stinking piece of cotton waste, seemingly untouched by everything and everyone around him. He was squeezing lice! He had just finished with his shirt, and was checking the wisps of hair in his armpits and the hair on his chest once more, to be sure, so that no little parasite should get away. Then with obvious pleasure he pulled the shirt over his head. He opened his trousers and started to search every seam, thoroughly, and calmly. All the while dispatch riders ran in and out, the wheezes of the dying continued, and heavy shells detonated so close to us that big pieces of cement fell from ceiling and walls. The noises trembled and sang in the head with the thunder and atmospheric pressure. Each time Schwarz found a louse, and there were plenty of them (here at the front we never got rid of them), he lifted it with a pleased grin against the weak light, snapped it with his nails, then let it fall down in the hot oil in the tin can. He did everything with calm, almost lazy movements.

Now and then Schwarz glanced furtively at the two dying men on the floor. He shook his head compassionately. Without any particularly dramatic accent, he turned and said to the officer by the radio "Do you see now that it's going to be hell for us?" Then he continued his raid among the lice.

Our new company commander came down to us. Schwarz rose to attention, with his trousers down. The newcomer, a sympathetic *Obersturmführer*, straight from Berlin, had not yet had time to become acquainted with Schwarz, a somewhat unusual officer. He was clearly surprised but received his report with a very straight face. It was clear that he had difficulty staying serious.

Then he caught sight of the bloody figures on the floor and knelt between them. He spoke in a low voice to them but got no other answer than the moaning, irregular wheezes. He whispered a question to the medical orderly and got a shake of the head as an answer. Then he stood up and gave a short, stiff salute to the two dying men.

Schwarz, with one hand holding up his trousers, went on reporting to the company commander. The *Unterscharführer* whom I had just relieved, went out to urinate. A roaring explosion was heard just outside the door. Covered with chalk dust, with his combat tunic in shreds, and scratches on his face and hands, he came rushing down again. His eyes were staring with fright and his body was shaking. From his stammering, disconnected and slurred speech, we understood that the shell had penetrated and destroyed the wall, a few metres from the entrance to the cellar, against which he had just urinated. He was completely finished. The company commander took him out and sent him to the rear as, together with his orderly, he left the cellar.

All night the Russian artillery heaved thousands of shells over our positions. My section of our company got its share, and it now seemed to me a wonder that our cellar had not collapsed from a direct hit and buried us. Towards morning the artillery fire increased even more, so that it sounded like an endlessly lengthy drum-roll, from which it was impossible to discern the single rounds. Trenches, bunkers and foxholes were ploughed apart by heavy shells that tore the crews to pieces. The firing was moved forward to make way for the advancing infantry forces. After bloody and close combat, hand-to-hand, in the ruined positions, they managed to break through in a couple of places. Our own side lacked the strength to force back the enemy, so we were ordered to disengage, and withdraw to new positions on the outskirts of Altdamm.

The retreat and occupation of the new positions was not followed by the combat pause we so badly needed. In an unchangeable, implacable onslaught the Russian artillery hammered on with its shells. Explosive bullets whistled uninterruptedly with devastating results. The struggle had changed character. Previously it had raged over fields and groves and through separate small villages. But now it rolled from house to house, from street to street.

The circle around the defenders of Altdamm was increasingly tightened. Everywhere Red Army soldiers swarmed forward and were shot to pieces. But they were followed by new waves. This yellow-brown throng was like a lemming migration. They fell in drifts. But over the corpses came new masses that raged without interruption, and without any sign of weakening. They waited around corners while the artillery, or the tanks, shot a defence 'nest' in a house to pieces. Then they rushed forth over the street, down into cellars, upstairs, and took the whole house, then on to the next. Was there no limit to their numbers?

Against this avalanche stood a fragile wall of completely exhausted men who were in mortal danger. They were SS men whose numbers shrank alarmingly day by day, even minute by minute. With the bitterness that characterised house-to-house fighting every man held out to the uttermost. The lightly wounded only gave themselves time to get a bandage at the nearest first-aid station, before returning to their combat positions. Every single man who still had the strength to keep himself up and handle a weapon fought with a fury that I had never seen before.

But our fighting strength grew weaker and weaker. More and more men were brought back bloody and torn, never to return, and no reserves came to fill the ranks. Only a thin line of hardened, determined veterans remained. They were hungry, deathly tired, bloody, many with bandaged arms or heads, unshaven, black from soot and smoke, mud and lime-dust, with uniforms torn to pieces. They felt their strength weaken but still determinedly clung to their weapons and aimed them with devastating effect against the seemingly endless assaulting forces.

After three days of furious fighting from house to house, orders finally came, on 20 March, to retreat over the Oder bridge. The situation had become very dangerous. The Red Army brought their main forces from the south, up along the banks of the Oder, to reach the bridge and with that, catch us in the bridgehead, as in a sack. In the afternoon, as the order reached us, we had managed to advance to a distance of only 300 metres, from the street that continued out on the bridge, our only way back. With superhuman effort the rest of our Division managed to stop their advance for some hours, and as darkness fell, the retreat started. By then the Bolsheviks had had time to correct the fire of their anti-tank guns against this most important street.

It became a case of 'running the gauntlet,' because their observers could see the flames from the exhaust pipes of our vehicles, as we clattered and rumbled at full speed towards the bridge. They aimed their guns at the flashes. For the crews in our vehicles it was many minutes of unbearable stress, driving through the danger area and over the bridge, until they reached the slightly safer Stettin side. But everything went comparatively well and the bridge was not blown up until the last men of the rearguard had crossed over.

The bridgehead at Stettin was a piece of German land drenched with blood, where some of the German fighting forces' best divisions desperately defended themselves against a wild assault by whole armies. But they had completed the task. The bridgehead had disappeared. Where the fighting had raged, fallen Russians were lying by the thousands.

Complete divisions of Stalin's élite had been brought there. But then they were annihilated in the furious defensive fire from exhausted, shredded, dirty but steadfast, 'field grey' men. Thousands of these brave farmers' sons, factory workers and young students, youth from all classes of society, had been left over there in the roaring, burning inferno, but it had cost the enemy a high price. Was this fight against the cruel, savage giant of the east the last battle, the 'Twilight of the Gods' of which the folks of our old Nordic faith had spoken? The Russian power of attack had petered out, the assault divisions were no more, and it took time to bring forward new forces.

For some weeks it became comparatively peaceful at the Stettin front. We who survived, with 'death' close behind us in the last minutes, had rushed back over the Oder and with our hearts in our mouths reached comparative safety on the other side of the bridge. Was it to be a repetition of the Napoleonic retreat over the Beresina, even if total disaster had not yet struck us? If only we had had half the enemies resources, half their tank and artillery numbers, or even half their enormous air armadas!

During a few days' rest we left behind us the task of stopping the flood for fresh troops. It threatened to crush the culture and work of generations and to make the people into slaves. From a formless grey crowd we gradually turned into thoroughly rested comrades. In front of us, a land spread out that just a few years before had seethed with the hopes of a strong, developing reconstruction. It had been borne on, and carried up, by a rare harmony between all national groups. This was a country, which, after its suffering, and through its re-born youthful enthusiasm and willpower, would waken a fading part of the world to new activity and wealth. From it would come scholarships, institutions, culture, and hardworking artisans and craftsmen from whom all humankind, for hundreds of years, would receive fresh impulses and fruitful ideas.

But now the country lay in unparalleled devastation. The Western allies of Stalin had carried on in a way that must have exceeded the old Eddas' most terrible fantasies. An unmerciful rain of phosphorus and high-explosive bombs had transformed and destroyed cities, modern industrial, commercial, and residential neighbourhoods. Their idyllic old districts, with half-timbered and step-gabled houses, some of them hundreds of years old, had been reduced to rubble.

Every night, defenceless, panic-stricken women, children and old people were killed in the glowing heat of the phosphorus rain, suffocated in firestorms. Millions of the survivors were made homeless and were forced out of a smoking and burning hell to a rootless roving life out on the roads. In the disorder children were separated from their mothers, wives from their husbands. Perhaps too, after this total chaos, they would never find each other again. Those who remained in the gaunt ruins were driven back thousands of years in their way of living. They became cave-people of our own time, with caverns and cellars as their homes. Despite all this, these people still held out in a situation that for years would not offer any chance of rejoicing or encouragement. They did not, and could not, give up hope of success in obtaining the right to live, free and equal as all other nations, after decades of degradation and humiliation.

The *Panzer Aufklärungs Abteilung* of Division Nordland, its armoured reconnaissance battalion, was now in poor condition. For the second time in six weeks, we rolled through Stettin, this time westward. In the city, ravaged by bombs, the Russian artillery had already started to complete the destruction that had been started by the British and American bomber armadas. Only very few civilians could be seen on the streets, but soldiers on the other hand were many. The preparations to meet the Red assault against the city itself were in full activity. Positions for the artillery were dug in the parks, and foxholes in the streets. Heavy trucks were positioned at street crossings, so that at the appropriate moment they would be used as barricades. Assault guns were dug in, and *Nebelwerfer* and mortars were brought into positions among the ruins. Above all this hung a black-yellow veil of smoke, coming from the violently burning Altdamm. Fires had also now started in Stettin and were spreading further and further.

All this we observed only mechanically. Neither eagerness nor energy lit up our eyes. We did not have the strength. Certainly we had felt terribly tired many times there at the front, but the tension, and the ever-present danger of death, had kept us up and going. It had worked as a stimulating drug, at a time when tiredness should have claimed its due long before.

As we now, temporarily, had managed to pull out of the 'jaws of death,' nerves relaxed again. Now we really became aware of how extremely tired and exhausted we were. Arms and legs felt heavy as lead, face and body ached. The mental tiredness made itself even more noticeable. It was impossible to complete a train of thought, to make a clear observation or a sober reflection. The exhaustion took the form of total apathy. The crews in the half-tracks sat slumped on their seats, thrown to and fro by sudden swervings. Even though they were thrown against the hard sides, they sank into a trance-like sleep. Everyone, chiefly the drivers and commanders of the vehicles, had to exert all their strength to take the long column to safety.

Wussow was the name of the place, west of Stettin, where the Division's supply unit was located. There the marching column split, and battalions and companies were separated into different camps. Apathetically, mechanically, platoons and groups took their positions at the formation area in front of a large farm. *Dienstausgabe* - the company commander gave the men orders as to what had to be done during the day and instructions were given about quarters, and such like. Of course, cleaning of weapons was essential before we could 'hit the sack'.

It was a trial to look over the weapons. A job that normally took only some minutes to do, now took half an hour or more. All the time we kept dropping small parts on the ground, out of pure exhaustion, just as they were ready to be assembled. Swearing, one had to clean them again. Or we sank into drowsing, indolently staring out into space, and could only with difficulty return to the present and continue the cleaning of weapons.

The men of the supply unit had arranged our quarters. Finally we were allowed to lie down in the straw. Just as I was about to sleep, after great difficulty in managing to take my boots off, a sooty face stuck out above my head. It was Ragnar Johansson II, also called 'The Giraffe,' the company commander's driver. He shook me roughly a couple of times before I really came round. At my cursing and protests he just grinned like a chimney sweep.

"You, hey, you, you've got a letter from home!"

If he had said that I had been awarded the Knight's Cross with Oak Leaves, Swords and Diamonds, I just would have turned and gone to sleep again, or perhaps before that have mumbled an uninterested 'really?' But this was something completely different!

"Where do you have it? From whom?"

Like a shot I was up from the barn floor.

"GP has it. He's by the 2nd platoon, but he'll soon be here."

In the semi-darkness I stepped on legs, arms and stomachs of sleeping comrades as I ran to the door. Damn, the boots! I had forgotten to pull them on. The same rough rampaging over the sleeping men again, of whom some now thought that it had gone too far and mumbled sleepy and blunt curses. It was impossible to get my swollen feet into the boots. I took the boots in one hand and ran out into the yard in my stockinged feet. Among the trees, where the vehicles of the 2nd platoon were standing behind the farmhouse, I spotted GP, who now had returned from the hospital, carefully wrapped in bandages.

"Give me the letter, GP!" I shouted.

He took a straddle-legged position, with his hands on his hips, and stared at me from top to toe.

"Is that the way you talk to a superior officer on duty? Stand to attention, man!" he bellowed. "I can see that you are dressed decently and according to regulations," he added with a diabolic grin and a sneering ogle at my feet.

He was standing there, making fun of me, shouting as would the meanest sergeant of the old school, who gave the recruits nightmares! But he could not hide the laughing twinkle in his eyes, and the mask did not last.

"Here's the letter," he said in a low voice, giving me a friendly push in the chest and going off to the next platoon.

It was the first letter from home for more than a year! It was from a girl back home who still kept me in her mind. The King's picture was on the stamps, and the postmark was from Stockholm. It was a little bit strange - I felt half ashamed of a lump in my throat. For more than a month the letter had been on its way from peaceful Stockholm with its cleanliness and, seen from the outside, its undisturbed life. It would still have its neon signs and friendly shining windows, with no 'black-out' curtains at night. Cinemas would be open and people strolling about. My letter had arrived in this only temporarily quiet corner, close behind a front where thousands of young men were killed or mutilated daily. It was a letter from another world!

I tore open the envelope with hands that now were shaking more from joyful excitement, than from exhaustion and the recent hardships' harrowing effects on the nerves. My eyes swept quickly over the lines. Then I read it again, slowly, then one more time, then once again.

Perhaps there was not very much in that letter. It was mostly about ordinary things and small events back home. But it strengthened and renewed me to think of life up there in the north. It was all so far away and distant from the life of the frontline soldier. It helped me to indulge in daydreams as I sat down outside the barn door. With the open letter in my hand, I started to think about how they were back home. For a year and a half I had not had a single line from home. Baffled, I had had to watch other fellow countrymen receive letters from Sweden, and hear them read, or tell the contents, during some pause in the fighting or marching. The letters that reached them were certainly more than a month old, and came with quite long intervals, but still they were connecting links to home that I had missed.

Just like the others, I had been utterly worn out. A week of long, uninterrupted combat action, without sleep, among collapsing houses, howling shells, and human beings torn apart in dirt, fire, smoke and blood, had consumed all our strength. The horrible sights had burned into our minds. All this, the tiredness, the apathy, and our broken, nervous condition had now suddenly disappeared. All thoughts of the previous days' experiences, and of war, had for the time being melted away. Now I was once again back home with my relatives and my friends. I was back in the well-remembered streets of Old town and the South side. My daydreaming went on until tiredness overwhelmed me, and I fell asleep just where I was sitting, still dreaming of far away Stockholm.

We were ordered even further to the rear, into rest areas, to recover from the latest hard fighting. It became one of those unforgettable recovery periods, between hard battles. It made us feel reborn and able to go into action with the old strength, as if it was the first time again. Orders became easy and possible. We performed an exercise now and then, so that we should not get too lazy. Otherwise it was mostly in our Swedish style, a little bit slow and rather like a not too strenuous training of recruits. Not like the usual double-quick speed of the Waffen-SS!

We had a good time, with lots of butter, cheese, eggs, ham and all the delicacies of the countryside. The farmers smiled contentedly at our appetite. Living conditions became comparatively luxurious in other aspects, too. One of our officers, for example, was very often impossible to find, since he had got to know a pretty beauty-expert, evacuated from Berlin - unless you cycled to the village where she lived and looked for him in the cave of the platinum blonde 'lioness!' There he probably enjoyed both manicure and pedicure and, most likely, more pleasant delights.

But when the company commander ordered formation, and attention, we all stood as statues. No one lost his style and became a *bon vivant*. Therefore Pehrsson could feel quite satisfied as he inspected, and stared every soldier in the eye. Polished to perfection, and exercised by the book, since after all, we were SS soldiers!

As well as all the *appells*, or as the Swedish army calls it 'visitations', we also had vehicle inspections. One such came particularly unfortunately, as far as I was concerned, a couple of days before the rest period was over. The crew of five of my half-track, myself modestly included, were quite successful 'organisers'. As we had a feeling that things would soon break out again, we had 'organised' quite a lot of suitable food from the kitchen and also in the way of clothes from the supply depot. Our vehicle was therefore so stuffed with canned goods of all kinds, butter, marmalade, underwear, et cetera, that it would have sagged if it were not for the armour.

Then came a bolt from the blue, an order of immediate half-track inspection. Not a chance to hide the treasures and prevent an ignominious confiscation! The *Spiess*, or company adjutant Hudeliest, in fact licked his lips, as he, together with the company commander looked down at all the 'goodies' to be seen through the hatch of our vehicle. He rubbed his hands in cruel voluptuousness and said "Doesn't it get cramped for you gentlemen in this 'cart'? I do believe that we must lift out some luggage, so that you can travel more comfortably."

Whereupon, with resigned sighs, we started to carry back all the goods to their point of departure. For me it was hardest to leave a pair of brand new boots, two sets of soft and nice underwear, a pair of nice short trousers of the new model and some socks. While I was getting the things together to carry them back to the supply depot, Pehrsson was standing up in the hatch of my half-track, peeping with a knowing face out into the blue, and drumming with his fingers on the armour. The *Spiess* was full of anticipation and helped me by taking the extra fine short trousers under his own arm.

The next morning Hudeliest came out of his quarters showing off in 'my' trousers. As he caught sight of me, he aimed his steps in my direction, stopped and said jovially "You don't mind me wearing 'your' trousers?"

I boiled and seethed inside, but he was a *Hauptscharführer* and I only an *Unterscharführer*, even if lately I had been entrusted with command over a platoon! Therefore I answered, trying to console myself, but with voice and face letting him understand that I behaved very generously to him "Of course not, *Hauptscharführer!*"

Well, we got some more 'peaceful' days, so that our vehicle did not contain just crew and regulation equipment when we got our marching orders!

# 7

# Küstrin

In the Stettin sector there had been comparative quiet since the withdrawal from the bridgehead. At that time, the Bolsheviks did not have the strength to advance over to the western bank of the Oder. Finally wiping out our bridgehead at Stettin-Altdamm had already cost them several of their best divisions. When such streams of blood had been shed, it took time to find new blood to 'drench' the soil of Pomerania. There seemed to be inexhaustible 'wells of Asia' to draw from.

Thanks to that, our position was quite safe for the time being. Upstream on the Oder it looked more threatening. Our entire defence depended on the Oder position. The Red Army brought forward enormous forces towards the sector between the Oder bend and Frankfurt, and began to feel their way around at different points.

As we began to sense trouble, the largest possible defence unit was made available. For instance, from the Stettin sector, they reinforced the positions that faced the Russians at the most threatened places. Our Division belonged to those that were sent southwards. We were ordered into position near the city of Schwedt, which lay right on the great Oder bend. After the transportation, and in the most wonderful spring weather, we had to start digging and building the positions at once. The very few civilians who were still there came voluntarily and helped us with the work, women as well as men. The sun was shining all day and despite the fact that it was only the end of March, it was as hot as in July. We did not hear much from Ivan, but there was a worrying, threatening anxiety in the air. After all, in Stettin we had seen with our own eyes what numbers the Russians managed to heave forth.

At that time, my mortar platoon was transferred to the 5th Company of our *Aufklärungs Abteilung*. Gradually we also heard, from other units that had fought their way back as far as from the Vistula, of strange events that clearly showed the Russians were now staking everything 'on one card' to try, with a single, powerful blow, to bring everything to an end.

We had experienced awkward situations before and were quite hardened, otherwise we should not have managed both the extreme psychological and physical strains of the retreat from Russia. That retreat took us far back into the old German territory. However, by then things were beginning to look ominous. Certainly, on our side, we knew that important things were going on, that sensational weapons would soon be put into action and, thanks to that, the war would take on a completely new character.

The new jet-propelled fighter-planes, which were far superior to the best British and American planes, were already in action and had caused heavy casualties among their bombers. We knew that even better things were coming. It was only a matter of time, a question of months. But could these months of respite be won? Would we be able to resist for long enough against such unbelievable masses? Supported by huge numbers of tanks, artillery and aircraft the Russians had numberless men. Such forces as those had never been seen before, and with violent, desperate force, day and night, all would be thrown against us.

If it were only the Russians! But in the west the American armies now swept in behind our backs with incredible speed. There, such things as hand-to-hand combat did not happen. It was an army of machines that stormed forth and broke the thin chains of brave, but exhausted defenders. The 'Yankees' did not take any unnecessary risks. For every little defensive line that had to be taken, even if it was just some small field fortifications and trenches with a hundred defenders, they first sent numerous bomber-planes that turned the whole area upside down. Then came just as many fighter-planes that with their machine-guns and rockets cleared the bomb-craters. At the same time the artillery sent a rain of shells over the unfortunate little piece of land. Not until then came the tanks, rolling forward in great masses. What was left of the defenders was, perhaps, some solitary human being, who could hardly manage to raise his hands above his head as the American infantrymen advanced to take the section.

Could we stand firm? Anxiety nagged inside us as, stripped to the waist and shining with sweat, we worked in the heat of the sun to improve our defensive positions. It must work! But the uncertainty, and the unanswered questions that darkened our minds, made us impatient and nervous. This uncertainty followed us everywhere, even at work in the trenches, during ever more frequent alarm-exercises, during pauses, and in our sleep.

It was little but perhaps useful consolation to have 'balanced the books' in one's life. The chance of surviving the war alive was so ridiculously small that one laughed just to think of it. My God, we had already seen so many men pass through this company! They had trod the hard and difficult way, from being recruits on the exercise field, to joining the replacement battalion, and on to the soldier's grave. It was impossible to keep them all in mind. It had to be several hundred, who marched with us in the 'silent' ranks of the company. Then why should we manage to get away with it? It was nothing to bother our brains with and that attitude gave us, curiously enough, more strength.

There was one man who, better than all the rest, felt and understood what was on the soldier's mind. He was the commander of the entire *Panzerkorps*, Felix Steiner, *SS-Obergruppenführer* and General of the Waffen-SS. We adored him, because he was a 'divinely' gifted leader and fighter. Many of us had already had him as commander during the days in the Wiking Division . He had risen through the ranks of command, and from divisional commander advanced to commander of the III *SS-Panzerkorps*, the Germanic *Panzerkorps*. Now he commanded this entire section and he knew his soldiers.

On Saturday 14 April he arrived unexpectedly. Certainly we had guessed that an exclusive visit was expected, as there had been extra strict polishing that day. We were taken by surprise, all the same, and were extremely enthusiastic at seeing 'the old one' come among us. He looked more serious than usual, as he stood in front of the company in its formation.

*Obergruppenführer* Felix Steiner was one of those talented leaders who are born, maybe, one in a million. A great feeling of calm, power and security always came from his robust and somewhat stocky figure. Every man who saw or heard him became part of this strength. He was tremendously hard and demanding, but at the same time he was as one with his people. It sounds hackneyed, and a bit of a cliché, that a commander should be like a father to his soldiers, but if something like that could be said about any officer, then it should be said of Felix Steiner. We adored him and were blindly devoted to him.

There he was, standing in front of us again as in the old days, and he spoke trustingly to us, man to man. He awoke memories from the days when we rolled forth across the vastness of Russia and beat Ivan wherever he offered resistance. He described the connection of 'causes' that had brought us here, to the frontline of the Germanic nations, and of the Occident against the Orient here in the Oder position.

He told us that in the presence of the greatest danger that had threatened western peoples and their culture since Attila and his Huns, these peoples were standing more divided than ever. Instead of facing up with united powers to ward off the new invasion, they were wasting their forces in devastating 'civil' wars. It had led to having only a part of Germany's armed forces as the most important defence against the threat of worldwide Bolshevism, facing the Barbarians. This force, because of devastating air-attacks against the homeland and its communications, had recently been able to gather only insufficient amounts of fuel, weapons and ammunition. He explained that our air force could not support us soldiers on the ground, as it ought, because it was constantly in action trying to protect our defenceless civilian population from the terror from the air. It seemed that the artillery and tanks we so badly needed could not come to us as fast as we required them, because railways, and other routes, had been destroyed by bombs.

"Whatever is to happen in the West, we must not think of it at present. The Oder front is the main thing. Just think! Here we stand, and with us stands or falls the entire Occident. If the Bolsheviks manage to force their way over, and swarm into the country, not only Germany is lost, the future destiny of the whole of Europe will be horrible. We must hold the Oder!"

After his speech he went along the front of the company, shook every man's hand and got every one to promise to do their utmost. There was more than one grim and hardened veteran who now suddenly felt a lump in his throat and a tear in his eye, as 'the old one' slowly went from man to man and quietly strengthened even more the feeling of unswerving brotherhood.

As he came to me, the serious, sharp features lit up in a shining smile. He had recognised me! And yet it was almost a year since I had participated in the delegation of all the Division's ranks, in Narva, that had congratulated him on his birthday. Since then he had, after all, seen innumerable faces of soldiers, but he remembered me. He even said my name. As if I was one of his close friends he asked me about what concerned me most, which was if I had heard anything from home lately. He asked how I had managed during the latest encounters and if I still got on well with my comrades in the Waffen-SS. I could not think clearly, everything went round in my head, and I only heard his friendly voice and saw his strong, clear, blue eyes looking at me. The surrounding comrades were just like a blurred background. Far, far away I heard my own voice, with a strange tone, answer the General's questions with a clarity that surprised me. As a 'farewell' he clapped my shoulder and said, with a glance that had gone fierce again "Yes, comrade, so far we have held out despite all strains. Now, more than ever, we all have to clench our teeth and stand firm, one for all and all for one!"

With a powerful handshake he went on, from man to man. All these tough men, voluntarily dedicated fighters to the death, who perhaps by then had forgotten the meaning of devotion, who in strained situations had learned to let coarse, grim humour be the power that kept up their courage in danger, were standing there filled with a peaceful devoted atmosphere.

Felix Steiner was a great soldier, divinely gifted, leader and comrade. We will never forget you! You were an inspiration and a brilliant holder of the unbreakable fighting spirit that, like a fanfare, sprang from the song the Waffen-SS had made its own, difficult, maybe impossible, to translate:

> *SS marschiert in Feindesland*
> *Und singt ein stolzes Lied*
> *Ein Schutze steht am Volgastrand*
> *Und leise summt er mit:*
> *Wir pfeifen auf unten, auf oben*
> *uns kan ja die ganze Welt*
> *verfluchen oder auch loben,*
> *genau wie es ihnen gefallt.*

It reflects the spirit of these tall, easy-going but steely disciplined boys and men, almost nonchalantly death-defying. It reflects their belief in the National Socialist classless society, where everybody had a fair chance.

It was the last time during the war that I saw *Obergruppenführer* Felix Steiner. Later, I heard that he had visited company after company, regiment after regiment, division after division. He had spread confidence everywhere and given incredulous and listless fighters new courage and new spirit.

Resting at Schwedt was an exceptionally calm and peaceful period. A violent struggle was going on a little bit further south, near Küstrin. With an unusual commitment of forces, the Bolsheviks tried to get a foothold on our side of the Oder. Their heavy assaults continued, without result, for some time. The countless shells from their superior artillery shot to pieces every other square metre on the defending side. They made the western bank of the Oder look like a lunar landscape. But, just as after every other artillery storm, when the Russian assault boats and amphibious craft set out from the eastern bank to hurry across, there were still German guns and machine-guns ready. The Russian crews were annihilated and their boats and amphibious craft were scuttled. In that way the slaughter went on, day and night. The stream was mixed with blood, and countless bodies were floating down the river.

If the Bolsheviks managed to get a foot on just an inch of the western bank of the Oder, there was a risk of great danger. Because of that the defenders fought with the greatest determination. It was a struggle where the reserves made the final result. Marshal Zhukov pushed forth everything he had. Divisions and armies from other sectors were ordered to Küstrin. Against this enormously heavy mass we had only some mobile units as reserves. All our forces were still badly needed at the places where they already stood.

Certainly the *Volkssturm* was obtainable as a last reserve, but they were only lightly armed and consisted mainly of older men who lacked youthful strength and persistence. Above of all artillery and air support were missing. What could we achieve, no matter how great the bravery, with only machine-guns, *Panzerfäuste*, mortars and anti-tank guns? We were up against an enormous enemy with tens of thousands of guns, thousands of tanks and Stalin organs, and a never-ceasing flow of fighter planes, that with rattling weapons and without mercy swept over the defence lines. Therefore the chain broke one day and the Russians set foot on the ground at the core of the Western nations, within the last natural border-barrier. From then on everything went forward with a raging momentum.

With fantastic speed the Bolsheviks started bridging the river, after their stormtroops had managed to advance some kilometres in each direction. But then they were stopped by promptly deployed reserves. Day and night Ivan worked feverishly to get over as great a force as possible, before a German counter-attack might come. As it went dark in the evenings searchlights were erected over the bridges and in their light the Russian pioneers could finish the work. However, the German air force, which was needed on the Eastern Front more than ever before, was involved in a struggle against the bomber armadas from the west. These dropped phosphorus and explosive bombs over defenceless civilians in the big cities of Germany. In Dresden, for example, the Allied bombers during three air raids within 20 hours killed as many as 200,000 civilians, mostly women, old people and children.

The Russian breakthrough had succeeded. The entire Oder front was in danger! Our Division, which was one of the fastest and most successful, was one of the forces that hastily was thrown forwards against that dangerous sector. We had to push back and liquidate the bridgehead. With a ruthlessly hard blow we should be able to throw the enemy into the river before he had taken too tight a hold.

Once again we rolled through the beautiful, fertile flat country softly undulating, its spreading groves, willow avenues straight as arrows, rich, well-managed farms, and magnificent castles. Something inside urged us on, to go faster! As long as we did not come too late! The responsibility urged us forward, towards the final confrontation. The short pauses were filled with anxiety, waiting for the next command. An order of the day from the Divisional commander made clear to every man in the ranks the gravity of the situation, and the importance of our own individual contribution.

All night long we continued in total darkness, without losing speed. The commanders of the vehicles, who always had their place standing behind the driver, had to direct them as they drove, as they had no chance of seeing the road. It was done with taps on one shoulder or the other, depending on how the road turned. It was quiet in our half-track, as quiet as it can be in a rattling and rumbling armoured vehicle. No one said anything, except for when the radio operator, to the right of the driver, with earphones attached, shouted a message from the company commander. If he turned the wavelength knob just a little bit he could also hear Russian commanders giving orders on the other side of the Oder.

At dawn on 19 April the information about the situation for every unit was completed and the orders given. We had to drive directly from the advance into positions of preparedness, to await the order for combat. Our *Aufklärungs Abteilung* was given as its position a village just behind the foremost lines, called Hohenstein. There we were left, together with another motorised unit, waiting for about 30 King Tiger tanks, which would connect up with us. Together with them we would launch a counter-attack.

The crews of the vehicles climbed out and spread over the whole village to stretch their legs and perhaps get a nap before the assault. I stayed with the driver in our half-track, standing by a barn, in which another half-track had been driven for protection from the sky. The village was full of soldiers, some like us, some from the *Wehrmacht*, and some from the *Volkssturm* whom I now, for the first time, would get a chance to see in front-line duty. Some of them were wearing uniforms, but many of them had just civilian clothes and a *Volkssturm* brassard. Their armament was mainly *Panzerfäuste* and submachine-guns. Their spirit was good, I guess, but how would these middle-aged and older men keep up, as the serious shooting started?

It was going to be satisfying, after so much infantry involvement, finally to get a chance to make a motorised attack. With the support of the King Tigers, our lighter vehicles should be able to penetrate deep into the bridgehead and create chaos with fast assaults among the advancing forces. In fact, after our experiences in the Baltic states, where we often had heavy casualties, we should have had enough of driving forward with our vehicles. But the last months of dismounting for infantry attacks all the time had awakened a new longing for armoured assaults. Yet we were not common infantry soldiers, but armoured *Panzergrenadiers* from the proud Germanic *Panzerkorps*, an elite unit dreaded by the Red Army and which others of our own armoured units envied.

The 30 King Tigers that were needed to break the Bolsheviks' barriers and make way for our own counter-attack to the Oder were expected at any moment. But there was still a little time for a short nap before the fight. It had become quite calm and peaceful in the village. Everyone had arranged a place to sleep in the best way they could, and the houses were full of sleeping comrades. Even I soon dozed away. The driver was already asleep in his seat.

A terrible thunder, as if the ground had opened for a volcanic eruption, woke us up with a violent shake and was followed by repeated close-up explosions in our immediate vicinity. I was up like a flash and stuck my head out through the hatch in the half-track.

It was a shocking sight! The previously peaceful village was, in an instant, turned into a hell beyond every attempt at description. Volley after volley from Stalin organs and heavy artillery created a horrible bloodbath. One after another the spray of continual impacts was thrown up from the village street. Houses were shattered and collapsed. Everywhere tongues of fire started to break out from windows and lick walls and roofs.

Soldiers jumped terrified out through doors and out of windows. Others came staggering with their hands on their bleeding heads or pressed against torn open bellies, where the guts came out through their fingers. Others shuffled with one or both legs cut off. But many were left inside the burning houses, dead or dying. Of those who managed to get out there was more than one who, after staggering just a few steps, sank to the ground never to rise again. Through the thunder of the shells rose desperate, wild death-cries and helpless groaning.

More and more of those who had been hit by the razor-sharp and red-hot shrapnel from the spouting fountains of earth fell and remained lying on the ground, coloured red-brown by growing puddles of blood. Soon the entire street was a mess of twisted bodies. The blood flowed in rills into the gutter. Hundreds of soldiers lay mangled and lacerated. In the middle of all this, shells continued to fall and tear to shreds even more bodies.

A bloody arm-stump hit with a splashing sound the side of the half-track, so that the blood splattered in my face. I had been standing motionless. As if hypnotised, I had been staring at the horrors that went on right before my eyes. The splatter of blood woke me up to activity. We must get out, away from the half-track! Rather take the risk of a shell splinter in the leg than stay in the vehicle and go up in the air with it. I bent down and yelled to the driver what to do. At the same moment a shell splinter hit the side of the half-track where I had been standing. I moved as fast as I could.

With the speed that fear of death gives, we jumped out of the vehicle and ran crouched towards a pit in the yard next to us. Then I saw that a shed, in which another of my platoon's half-tracks stood, was on fire. The sense of duty, which remains with you even in the worst of situations, forced me to run over there.

The barn was already full of smoke. Coughing and cursing, I climbed down to the driver's seat. Damn it! No matter how much I tried, with my nervous, shaking fingers, I could not get the motor started. It howled and whistled in the air. Close to the barn there was a heavy explosion that sang in my head and fire sparked up alarmingly. I jumped out again! From the hatch opening I saw my driver lying in a cemented water trough peering in my direction. Suddenly he disappeared behind a black-brown pillar of whirled up earth and shell splinters. 'Finished!' I thought. No, he was still alive, unhurt in his strong shelter. I waved wildly at him. Instantly he came running. Down! A new shell explosion, then up again and forwards, but down again! Through the whipping rain of shells he reached me, gasping.

"I can't get it started!" I shouted. "You try, but hurry up, before we are blown to pieces."

He wriggled down there inside, cursed wildly, wriggled some more and got the motor started. One of our best drivers!

"Drive as fast as you can! I'll take our own half-track!" I shouted to him, and ran off.

With a quick glance over my shoulder I saw the vehicle trundle out of the burning barn and roll away. Stumbling over fallen comrades, and time after time taking cover from howling shells, my face pressed down in puddles of blood, I forced myself towards the barn, behind which I had left my own vehicle. There was no point staying in this slaughter-house any longer, where every minute survived was a miracle. The whole village was already burning violently and the heat created a heavy draught of smoking flakes and stinging showers of sparks. There was no co-ordinating hand anymore, only fallen, wounded, and occasional survivors who in panic tried to save themselves from the hell around us.

Of the entire force that should have been the battering ram against the Bolsheviks' bridgehead, nothing but shredded remains was left. The attack had been smashed to pieces before it even started. Our recce battalion, an elite unit with only few counterparts on the entire Eastern Front had had one of its bloodiest days of the whole war. All this had happened in only about 30 minutes, if that long. In situations like those, one lost the ability to measure time.

Covered with the blood of fallen comrades I ran round the corner of the barn. Our half-track was gone! Someone from the crew must have made it out of the rain of shells and driven away, understandably believing he was the only one left of us. But there I was out in the open! I did not know where the battalion might reassemble in this confusing, chaotic situation. At the same time it was quite easy to guess that very soon the Bolsheviks would be coming with both tanks and infantry, after this violent preliminary bombardment. And the fire was not only in this village. The thunder was heard on all sides. A major attack was going on!

From the far end of the village some men came hurrying. A wounded man with a bloody bandage round his head was led, half-running, between two comrades. It was clear that they came from the front line. Without taking any notice of the shell splinters flying around they kept on at a staggering run. One of them fell, his head had been torn off and the blood squirted like a fountain from his throat. Another had his leg sliced off above his knee and he shuffled away on his elbows. There was no chance of helping. No medical orderlies were to be seen. They had probably been torn to pieces, too. Anyone who was left on the village street was finished.

The nearest one in a small group of infantrymen from the *Wehrmacht* shouted, as he caught sight of me through the smoke. I was lying, scarcely protected, behind the stone base of one of the burning houses:

"The Ivans have broken through over there!" he shouted. "Lots of them are coming!"

Now I was running, too! Leaping over the fallen, I ran with a pistol in my hand towards the only way out. Red Army soldiers could show up at any moment and I was prepared to sell my life as dearly as possible.

In a passing glance I saw a sight which burned into my mind forever. In the middle of the street an old *Volkssturm* soldier was sitting. His silver-white hair was bloody from a wound on his skull. His *Panzerfaust* he had lying beside him. A wounded young SS soldier's deathly pale head he held in his lap, and stroked, with a gentle hand, over the forehead and cheeks that were turning yellow. The SS man had had both his feet torn away. He was doomed, but still it was terrible to meet his appealing, pleading look in that flashing glance and then to rush on without being able to take him with me. If I had stayed, none of us would have got out of there alive. Moreover, he would have bled to death before I could carry him a hundred metres.

In wild speed I kept on running. The exhausted *Wehrmacht* soldiers, who did not have the strength to keep up with me, lagged far behind. But, no matter how I ran it seemed impossible to get out of the rain of shells. It seemed to move forward at the same speed as I was running. Finally, beyond a narrow forest belt it became a little quieter. But behind me it thundered, howled and crashed. It was a bombardment that went on like a giant steamroller and crushed everything under its weight.

The dam had broken. Like a balloon that bursts, the Red Army bridgehead at Küstrin finally broke through the German defence line. There had been several days' build-up of great masses of troops who were held in that limited area. With this enormous power, practically undisturbed from the air, day and night they had been taken over the river. The blow aimed at the short sector grew to devastating dimensions. I already realised that the Oder front was lost. The words of *Obergruppenführer* Steiner rang in my ears. "How shall all this end?" asked myself time after time, while with burning throat and wildly thumping heart I ran over the field, towards a small group of armoured vehicles standing in a clump of trees.

They were some of our own. The company's adjutant was in command. It was he who, together with the driver from another knocked out half-track, had taken mine and driven here. The company commander was a new one who had been sent to replace the wounded one, another had been killed, and there were two wounded platoon leaders. The company adjutant, Hudeliest, had stayed there to pick up possible late-coming survivors. He told me that twelve men of my platoon had been killed in the village and that my driver, together with the half-track we had saved from the burning barn, had been sent into the air by a direct hit right before his eyes. Of the mortar platoons' ten half-tracks, four were left – with reduced crews! In that short moment we had lost more men than during several days' violent fighting in Stettin.

Men from the shattered frontline now started to emerge from the edge of the forest. We ran towards them and took care of those in worst condition. They were totally exhausted and shocked. As many wounded as we possibly could take on our half-tracks, were helped to hold on. The most badly wounded were put on the almost horizontal flat bonnets. The others followed running, as we drove on to join the main force of the depleted recce battalion. At least it gave them some feeling of returning strength and courage. Following the tracks of the armoured vehicles gave them a small sense of security.

Having reached the nearest road, we managed to stop some empty ambulances, which took care of the wounded *Wehrmacht* soldiers, and we could carry on alone. My vehicle was quite badly damaged and needed a thorough overhaul and repair at the nearest repair unit. It was possible to drive, even if it was not up to much. Yet, we were able to follow the other vehicles, although we could not maintain the same speed.

That was how it came about that suddenly we were alone, in the middle of a unit from the *Wehrmacht*, under the command of a *Major*, with the Knight's Cross and a hard, hot-tempered look. I had noticed him earlier in the morning in the village, where he commanded the motorised unit that together with us had had its frontline position there. Obviously he had now raked together all those able to fight and those that he had managed to stop among the retreating. He was now fully occupied grouping them for defence in a wide semi-circle – out in the middle of the field! The Soviet attack-fighters would 'lick their lips' when they caught sight of them, and that probably would not take too long.

With his chin in a brutally advanced position, and a pistol in his hand, the *Major* ran around chasing the men. This was murder and suicide! As he saw our half-track come slowly lurching along, he rushed towards us and gave the signal to stop. You could tell from his face that an armoured vehicle was just what he considered he needed. The driver stopped the vehicle and the company's adjutant, Hudeliest, who was sitting on the top, while I was standing in the hatch-opening, asked calmly and without any introductory words of politeness, what it was all about. In the Waffen-SS respect for officers from the *Wehrmacht* had never been overwhelming and an Iron Cross 1st Class in the Waffen-SS was ranked almost as high as a Knight's Cross of an officer of the *Wehrmacht*. You could see on the *Major's* face that the nonchalance of the adjutant made him furious.

"I guess you are running away!" he roared.

"Oh no, we are just going to join our unit," the adjutant answered, still sitting on the half-track.

"If you don't come down from that vehicle at once, and stand to attention when you speak to me, I'll make a hole in you!" the *Major* growled, and waved the pistol.

The adjutant and I exchanged a quick glance. You could tell from the *Major's* look and his angry bright red face, that he meant what he said. The adjutant jumped down from the vehicle, stood to a stiff attention, saluted and reported:

"*Major*! I am adjutant of the 4th Company, *Aufklärungs Abteilung*, SS *Panzergrenadier* Division 'Nordland' with two men, and a half-track of the mortar-platoon, under transportation to the collection point of the company."

"I need you here. You will be put in as fire-support. Await orders from me!" the *Major* said and turned around to continue the grouping of the defence.

"*Major*! The vehicle in its present condition is useless. It has to be, according to orders, taken to the nearest repair-unit for repair," the adjutant dared to object.

The *Major* rushed back towards us.

"You stay here and await my orders!" Then, he left.

The adjutant climbed up on the half-track again. This was a nice prospect! Everywhere violent sounds of battle could be heard and the thunder of artillery came closer. And there, in the middle of the field, stood some hundred men without any protection at all. A sweep from a fighter-plane, or a well-aimed set of shells, and there would not be very much left of us.

The adjutant did not say a word, just glared grimly after the *Major* who was rushing away. As the *Major* reached the furthest flank, about 300 metres away from us, the adjutant leaned down into the half-track and said to the driver "Drive as fast as this thing can!"

Growling, the half-track shook away. It was not cowardice.

"No one has ever yet dared to accuse me of that and I do not think there has been a reason to do so either. On one hand we have to join the company before the Bolsheviks turn up everywhere. On the other hand we do not want to be killed in such an ignominious way without a chance to hit back."

The adjutant muttered all this to me as we hung out from the hatch-opening and peered in the direction of the *Major*, who still had not noticed our retreat from his insane 'defence' line. We felt sorry for the men there.

We had come perhaps 300 metres away from there, when an unpleasant, all too familiar howling was heard. Stalin organs! Instinctively you pull down your head between your shoulders.

Bull's-eye! Right in the middle of the force of men. The salvo from the terrible weapon gave such a total result as only Stalin organs or German *Nebelwerfer* can attain. We saw black-brown earth, and human bodies, whirl up through flashing explosions, that came one after another. As the black dust settled, not a movement was seen among the soldiers there. The horrible work of an instant!

We looked at each other. We were there just a minute before! Once again 'luck' and the unfathomable instinct that warns the frontline veteran had given us a hand.

Beyond the field we reached a meandering road that we followed. Suddenly the fighter-planes came! Repeatedly, they came down over the road and the fields, where swarmed even closer numbers of vehicles and retreating soldiers. Like a scythe the hail of bullets whistled over men and vehicles. Each time one such 'monster' came roaring, we threw ourselves into the interior of our half-track. They gave us no peace. It grated on our ears and made our entire bodies ache at the sound of their howling engines. Increasingly we passed burning vehicles and entire rows of fallen soldiers who had not got far enough away from the road to escape the projectiles. But once again we were lucky. The assault whistled and crackled around us. We crouched down and tried to think of something else, and at last the attack was over. So it continued innumerable times.

In a bend stood *Standartenoberjunker* Schwarck. We picked him up and moved on. After the company commander had been wounded, Schwarck, only 20 years old, had been given the command of the 5th Company. He had stayed to try to find us in all the chaos, and take us back to the supply unit.

About 50 metres from the road an 88mm gun was standing. Stripped to their waists in the sunny weather the crew worked frantically. The sweat shone on their backs, as they ran forth with the shells, loaded and fired in a steady, fast pace. From the sky a Soviet fighter-plane suddenly came diving like a falcon. The engine noise and the whistling air-stream warned the artillerymen, who without any sign of panic ran away to their protection trench after having sent off the shell that was already in the barrel. Like an arrow the plane dived down at the gun placement. The engine noise grew louder with the dizzying speed to a deafening, frightening howl. Just a hair's breadth over the gun, the plane dropped a bomb, turned its nose a few metres over the ground up into the sky, and climbed with fantastic speed and disappeared.

The bomb missed its target by about 30 metres, threw up a mushroom-shaped cloud of earth, but did no harm. The artillerymen rushed out of their protection trench, shells were brought out, put in the barrel and the firing continued mechanically, as fast as after a short break on the exercise field.

It had been a short but fascinating *intermezzo*. What an amazingly gifted pilot, what a dive! And what hardboiled, steel-hard fighters were these anti-aircraft gunners, who only unwillingly it seemed, ran away from their position. Immediately after the bomb exploded they ran back and continued the fast firing as if nothing had happened!

Under Schwarck's command we drove past long caravans of retreating units and gradually reached the supply unit and re-joined the company. Many familiar faces were missing, of men who that very morning had smoked my cigarettes or borrowed my pipe tobacco, with whom for months the fortunes of life had been shared, and who had kept clear heads in many dangerous situations. The gaps were terrifyingly large and as *Standartenoberjunker* Schwarck ordered us to form ranks, it appeared that about half of the men were gone, most of them killed. Of the wounded, only those with more serious wounds were absent. Everyone who could still walk, stand and handle a weapon had returned from the nearest first-aid station after having been given a meagre bandage. Felix Steiner would have had his heart warmed if he could have seen these thinning ranks of smoke-blackened, dirty SS men with torn uniforms, many with bloody bandages, but everyone ready for new engagements. The horrors of the morning had shaken but not broken us. We still had weapons and ammunition!

Orderlies hurried here and there, dispatch riders drove back and forth on highways and on sandy village roads. Meanwhile, rumours flew around. Contradictory information went from mouth to mouth, was answered and denied. For everyone thought it was clear that the general offensive against Berlin had opened. Certainly we had not been in the extreme foremost frontline and seen them coming. But the violence of the artillery hurricane and the enormous forces of bomber and fighter-planes had shown and told us clearly that this was the prelude to the hour of decision.

Out on the roads, chaos ruled. Every crossroad, every little railway station and every bridge was showered with bombs, and over the marching columns the projectiles rained down from the fighter-planes. Tanks, cannons, trucks, ambulances and tractors were heaved around and mixed in confusion with dead horses and the twisted bodies of fallen soldiers and torn off limbs. More and more often traffic jams occurred, and on the compact masses the bombs had a terrible effect. To run away from the roads helped only a little, because around them spread only arable land and fields, with only occasional small groups of trees here and there. The bombs did the heavy work and the fighter-planes searched thoroughly. They hunted in wide sweeps and sharp turns at thirty, twenty, even ten metres' height, after the fleeing soldiers. Out in the fields their projectiles ploughed long furrows in the ground. The bursts of gunfire raged amongst the running men until they fell, and remained still.

In the middle of this bloody confusion the staff of the Nordland Division were stunned and chilled. The scattered battalions and companies were gathered and made ready for action. The front had really come into being and it did not take long before we got combat contact with the Red Army once again. It was a repetition of the exhausting battle of Pomerania. Everywhere the Bolsheviks turned up before we knew anything. There was no limit to their tank forces. The infantry we saw less of, though. It was with material superiority that they would break us now. Time after time it happened that we, involved in combat, realised that the forces we had against us consisted exclusively of tanks, assault guns and entire battalions of Stalin organs. There was not one infantry soldier among them. The motorization of the Red Army had reached its peak. The infantry were obviously mostly transported on American trucks, following in the tracks of the tank units.

The struggle was furious and our losses were heavy. Our Division soon had not much more strength than a regiment. As orders came that this or that company should go into position to defend a sector of the terrain, it was not unusual to see an *Untersturmführer* take a machine-gun on his shoulder and move off together with an *Unterscharführer* and a couple of men who carried the ammo-boxes. And that was the whole company! What could we hope to achieve with battalions of forty to fifty men, and regiments with two or three hundred? But we continued fighting! Into position, a short fight, then up again and away. We would be suddenly surprised by fire from behind, find ourselves surrounded but somehow come out and be back in combat again! So it went on continuously, without sleep, and almost no food, for days.

Ivan, who always used to avoid assaults at night, now kept on moving uninterruptedly round the clock. It felt weird, to hear the tank engines' dull growling continue through the dark, to see the muzzle-flashes, and to hear the Bolsheviks' battle cries. Our strength was strung out to an extent that one might almost say was superhuman. But for every position that we were forced to abandon, the enemy paid a high price in their fallen.

During those first days after the catastrophe at Küstrin, we never saw soldiers from other units than our own division. It seemed as if the whole burden was on our shoulders, but of course other units close to us fought the same desperate struggle against those superior forces. As we hovered between life and death in those days, we did not have time to think about such things. For a platoon leader there was not even the possibility of any general view, even within a narrow sector.

We fought, ran, drove, dug in, fought, ran and drove on again, all without pause, without ever getting out of the iron grip. It was so exhausting and took our strength so completely, that no separate events remained in our minds. It just became a continuation of mixed and confused sights of shell explosions, burning tanks, farms, and cities. We saw villages in smoking ruins or blazing bonfires, dying comrades to the right and to the left, and we heard their mournful groaning and piercing cries of pain. We saw bearded, dirty, bloody, soldiers' faces with red-rimmed eyes.

I do not know for how long we had been alone against these superior forces in our sector, but at last other units began to come to our aid. Certainly there was no time for proper and much needed rest. But at least we had time to get our breath, now and then, between the fights. We could sometimes stretch out for half an hour before waking up to a new engagement. We were sick from the tiredness that lay like lead over body and brain. The tension would sometimes ease. Then we might just have time for a short nap.

Sometimes we had time to rush into some farm when passing, to eat some of the food that perhaps was standing untouched on the table. Sometimes food was still on the stove, hardly cold. Sometimes clothes and household utensils were still in place, as if the owners had left the rooms just for a short while. However, in the cowshed the cattle were 'mooing' and on the porch the cat was sitting, licking its paws in the sun. The high speed of the Red offensive in these surroundings had made the escape of the civilians panicky and precipitate. In tragically many cases the fleeing were caught up and captured, or murdered, by the Bolsheviks. These swarmed in everywhere behind the defenders, who no longer managed to keep a continuous line.

Among the new, incoming troops there were plenty of *Fallschirmjäger*, men of the right, tough stuff who brought with them the responsibilities and memories of Crete, North Africa and Monte Cassino. They knew their work. In other places close to us Walloon and French SS volunteers fought with Gallic bravery. The speed of the offensive was slowed down a bit, but we never managed to create an unbroken defence line. Too often, newly built up defence positions were knocked out by some of the Bolsheviks' strong tank spearheads that succeeded in penetrating deep into a sector. Our own minor reserves, that should have been put into action with a chance of success in some other place, had to be thrown there hastily, with the result that the sector from which the rescue had come was cut off by some other tank assault. In that way, the Russians bored their route towards the west through surroundings that within a few hours were transformed from fertile peasant country to devastated steppe.

More than once we had to withdraw hastily from some resistance 'nest', because the Bolsheviks attacked our rear by coming in on our flanks. In such cases valuable equipment had to be abandoned. In exceptional cases it was possible, by retaking the lost terrain, to take back the equipment before the Bolsheviks had destroyed it or taken it out.

# 8

# A Gauntlet

I made such an attempt to bring back lost equipment, together with two mechanics, in one small town. It had been lost in the early morning but, later the same day, had been recaptured by our *Fallschirmjäger*. During the headlong retreat that morning our *Aufklärungs Abteilung* had to leave an assault gun behind in the ruins. It had some engine problem and could only drive backwards! However, it was standing in such a bad position between a couple of badly damaged houses that it was impossible to get it out as we withdrew. There was no time to repair it but I thought that it was a shame if an otherwise faultless and ready-for-action vehicle should be lost and fall into the hands of the Bolsheviks. So I took two mechanics, and in a heavy Steyr car, an excellent and far superior German version of the American jeep organised from a *Wehrmacht* depot, we drove back towards the town. For all emergencies I brought Walter Leisegang, one of the most reliable men in the platoon, and, of course a machine-gun.

We drove straight towards the roar of battle. Obviously we had to hurry up, before Ivan had time to refresh and attack again. It was an unpleasant surprise when we discovered that the worst thunder and crashing came from the target of our expedition. We did not worry too much about the belching of smoke over the town, because it had been burning since the previous evening, as the Russian artillery had started playing its 'preludes'. The risk was that the Russians were already back in the town.

A few hundred metres from town we met two *Fallschirmjäger* who came carelessly trotting along as if on a Sunday outing, with their pipes dangling in their mouths, cartridge-belts over their shoulders and small dust-clouds whirling around their marching-boots on the sandy little by-way.

I slowed down and asked what it looked like over there. "Is it Ivan shooting in town?"

"No, it's our own tanks firing. No risk so far," they both explained convincingly with one voice and continued their Sunday-like walk.

"Well, let's carry on then, lads," I said and we drove off.

Certainly it was easy to figure out that the Bolsheviks could not be too many hundred metres beyond the town, but they were not there yet.

It was clear though, that we had to hurry up before they came. Full throttle!

With maximum speed we drove in on the main street, and as fast as possible wove between the shell craters, among blown up horse-carriages and anti-tank guns that Ivan had left during his retreat. There was no lack of fallen Russians. They were lying everywhere like brown-yellow bundles in strange positions. As we went I could see three *Fallschirmjäger* with a *Panzerschreck* behind a partly ruined fireproof wall. Even if they did not rub their eyes, they looked surprised, to put it mildly. They waved eagerly and shouted something at us, but we were in a hurry and did not have time to listen.

With an elegant turn we stopped in the town square with flowers at the edge of a small pond. In peaceful, happier days, this was the playground of the town's children with slide, swing and sandpit. I guessed that a week or only a few days ago blonde-haired children played here and filled the air with their joyful laughter. Today they were probably fleeing on the roads westward, chased by American fighter-planes or lying in ditches with blood in their hair. Today the swings stood empty, reminding us of the Russian invasion. Other sounds filled the air, not soft and playful, but hard and shrill. The soft lawn with fresh greenery and flowerbeds with blazing spring-flowers were badly damaged and the young trees were broken and splintered by shells. The smoke lay like a poison-cloud over the once idyllic, but now pockmarked plantation.

There were powerful rumbles here and there in the town. Running, we crossed the square, turned in on a side street and worked our way up the quite steep hill. Up there on the crest, squeezed in between the houses stood the assault gun, which we could repair and bring back with us. The long barrel, pointing eastwards, stuck out from the row of houses. No soldiers could be seen, but rumbles and clanking sounds could be heard. Otherwise the town seemed dead. Just before we reached the crest, we heard the clatter of tanks from the other side.

"Move, men! Our tanks are starting to withdraw!" I shouted over my shoulder to the others.

Just then a tank appeared and heaved itself up on the crest in all its splendour. I stopped dead. Hell, am I right? That long barrel, that turret – it was a Stalin tank! There was a 'click' in my head and my heart jumped into my throat.

"Get back! It's Ivan!" I shouted and started running down the hill, head over heels.

Up there they were not as surprised as we were, because before we had run many metres the first shell came whistling between the houses. We ran as if on fire, but it became worse! The shells whined and howled between us and above us, and the opening in the street was down there like a distant mirage. Fright gave us wings, as with heads down we rushed along the cobbled street. At every dull bang from up there, the heart contracted but their direct shooting did not succeed and the shells hit somewhere on the other side of the square. Then they started shooting diagonally at the house walls to reach us with splinters. These whistled painfully around our ears and clinked against the pavement. My left sleeve was ripped open by a splinter, one of the mechanics had his hand torn to pieces, so that the blood sprayed as he ran in front of me with swinging arms. But we got away!

At last! With an extra effort we threw ourselves around the corner of the square, at the same moment as a window came crashing down. No further order was needed to get the men running at full speed towards our car by the pond. I happened to glance to the left and saw Bolsheviks with submachine-guns come walking, quite light-heartedly, along the house walls, from the eastern half of the main street towards the square. Then I began to realise what the *Fallschirmjäger* behind the fireproof wall shouted at us, as we came: "The town is in the hands of Ivan!" Had they seen us over there? In that case we could say 'goodbye'.

As we ran over the lawn, I could see that a brown-yellow figure stood tampering curiously with the machine-gun in the car. Before he could react, I got my pistol up and he sank over the gun. Up in the car! Walther threw the Bolshevik aside. He was a small Kirghiz with flat face and slanted eyes. We jumped down in the backseat with the machine-gun over the edge. The mechanic with hands unhurt was ready with the submachine-gun. At full speed we rounded the pond and set off towards the way out. The Bolsheviks at the other end of the square came running, but Walther kept them down with the machine-gun. A patrol, which sneaked forward in our direction, was so surprised as we slid, jumped and whined past, that they did not think of shooting. But Walther and the mechanic did and the Russians fell like puppets.

The pungent smell of smoke disappeared and the air was blowing freely around us again. We were out of the town, leaving it and the Bolsheviks behind us at increasing speed. Not until then did we feel the exertion. The sweat ran down our backs and hot faces, finding its way into our eyes, smarting from the saltiness, and flowing into our mouths.

We all panted with the excitement and tension that did not let go until we were back at the supply unit.

There, urgent preparations for combat were going on. We were to be sent into action again. Our company, which after all had managed better than most in the Division, now numbered not more than 40 men. The indescribably hard days after Küstrin had cost us more, good, brave comrades than during many months earlier in the campaign. Now, those times seemed to be over for ever, when after a hard engagement we could withdraw behind our lines for a week or at least a few days, to refresh ourselves and recover before returning with renewed strength. The word 'rest' did not exist for us any more. There was only engagement, engagement, and more engagements, with very fast energy-sapping troop movements in between.

After all that had happened we should by now have been used up, finished, 'over and out'. But we clenched our teeth and forced ourselves on to even greater struggles. We went on automatically, without any time for reflection, but on pure instinct of the sort that helps the frontline soldier to survive, when theoretically he should be dead, either by bombardment, close combat or ambush. The brain could not take in anything more while in this state of exhaustion. Not until now had we fully shown the meaning of a defiant fighting spirit, or of a burning conviction and knowledge of a clear cause for struggle, all of which are needed by the frontline soldier. Without this he can certainly fight, especially when he has superior artillery, aircraft and tanks in support. But in adversity, in the face of an apparently invincible enemy who has countless material assets, and without support from his own side's heavy weapons, he collapses and longs for captivity.

# 9

# A Spark of Hope!

When you are in practically uninterrupted engagements in the foremost frontline, without contact with the outer world, and with days and nights melting together into a continuous crescendo of bombardment, close combat, and nerve-racking experiences, there is no possibility of measuring time. It is as if the wheel of time had stopped and the present were eternal.

It seemed impossible to escape from the present. In our case it was completely filled with nervous strain, shocks and frightening sights. Single events, in the long chain of fateful days and nights, were mixed together into one huge, unreal picture of horror, where even today it is difficult to separate the details. The general impression that remains today, from that bloody April 1945, is the feeling of a lonely warrior's desperate final struggle. Almost disarmed, and bleeding from countless wounds, we found ourselves up against an enemy of unlimited resources.

We were getting closer to Berlin. The landscape changed character. We drove into the pine forests of Mark Brandenburg, where small lakes glittered between the trees. Weekend cottages, taverns, and small refreshment inns for cyclists and motorists who used to come from Berlin on Sunday trips became more and more numerous. Now they were empty, or temporarily lodged wounded and exhausted soldiers. On the gable of an idyllic little tavern close to the highway, we met the blazing words *Berlin bleibt Deutsch!* ('Berlin remains German!') They were painted over the bleached wall-advertisement for the beer brand *Berliner Kindl.*

When we saw the words for the first time it gave us a deep feeling of fatefulness. The struggle was drawing to its end. Now or never the fortunes of war had to turn. If not, everything that after years of deprivation, hardship and indescribable mental strain we had voluntarily fought for, would collapse in chaos. It would be without equal in the history of mankind.

*Berlin bleibt Deutsch!* What a road was behind us, as now we stood facing this last, defiant, fighting talk! Once, we had stormed forth victoriously over the boundless plains of east Europe. With the fighting excitement of youth we had thrown ourselves into battles that have gone down in history. Many of us, after the assault over the Kuban and Terek rivers by Malgobek and Maikop, could have imagined Asia beyond the cloud-topped, snow-covered Caucasus.

Well, perhaps we were not so many now, since most were now 'resting in the earth' between Asia and the suburbs of Berlin. Would any of us get through to the end? Who dared to still believe in the 'genius' of the soldier's luck? We were in the company of some, who already had been standing under its protection, and had repeatedly, thanks to miracles, been saved from death. However, at some time, the last straw would be drawn for each one of us and a soldier's death would come.

Our spirits had sunk steadily during the last days, and had come dangerously close to zero. Here in the forests of Brandenburg, we now met a new enemy. Roving armed gangs of Polish and Russian civilians began to show up at night, to rob and plunder. Frequently they attacked smaller units of our Division. They were beginning to escape from their camps, find weapons, and were now trying to correct their personal records for a proper alibi at the prospect of the approaching Red Army.

These were individuals who had been transferred from a miserable existence in Belorussian and Ukrainian hovels, filthy, stinking, lice- and flea-filled mud huts, and had been hired to work in the German war industry. For the first time in their grey hopeless lives they had encountered well organised work places and humane living conditions. Their dirty and flea infested clothes had been replaced by clean overalls and real underwear from the already scares supplies of their 'host' country, though after unaccustomed hot, soapy showers and disinfectants that made their lice and fleas swim away into no-no land. Now they called themselves *sklaven arbeiter* - slaves; but they had been paid, decently housed in spartan barracks, and had been fed with their accustomed regional food from collective kitchens in clean mess halls. There had been nightly entertainment for them - theatre performances in their mother tongue, evenings with music both classical and folk, and variety shows. Gradually they had learned to use soap and water on a daily basis and other elementary concepts of personal hygiene. In short, they had begun to live like human beings.

They were now hardly any danger to us, but their behaviour gave us a clear hint of what, in those days, was the situation behind the front. This contributed to the depression on our spirits. There could no longer be any doubt that the authorities had begun to lose control over the situation on the home front. These were bad signs.

In the middle of this heavy depression new rumours suddenly began to circulate. They popped up here and there and spread like wildfire from man to man. Soon after the first intimation had come up in the Divisional staff, everybody knew. The rumours that woke us up from our mechanical, trance-like, defensive fighting, and gave us new hope, and new spirit, said that *Reichsführer-SS* Himmler had contacted the supreme commander of the western allies, Eisenhower. It was said that he, after having heard Himmler's narration of the 'Red danger', had realised the equally great effect on the British and Americans of this danger. It was a danger to the whole West. They now had now supposedly agreed about common struggle against Bolshevism, before the Red Army reached Berlin.

At last! Year after year the greatest Germanic peoples had been in bitter, bloody feuding with each other. They sacrificed their best youth in wars between brothers, while their common enemy had taken advantage of the situation to force his way deeper into Europe. Now, in the darkest hours of the West, the previous adversaries could have joined in facing the imminent threat. It was too wonderful to be true! But we believed, because what else should we believe in and hope for, there, a few miles from the heart of the German capital? We found new strength, tightened our helmets and fought with new determination. We no longer had the attitude of the death-sentence, to sell your life as dearly as possible, but instead, we went on cheerfully and hopefully, like those certain of victory.

What then did it matter if the agreement, in other respects, could perhaps be humiliating for Germany? That was something relative. The main thing was that all forces came together right then. Closer than to the gates of Berlin the Red Army should not be allowed to come! And they could not do that if the British and Americans joined us. Certainly it would be enough if just our own comrades in the west could be made available and come to our help. We would hit the Bolsheviks outside Berlin, chase them eastward, annihilate the entire Red Army, and smash the Soviet regime to pieces, so that it should never be able to rise again.

These were prodigious thoughts! They had been lying smouldering in the subconscious during the difficult years of constant retreat and had kept the fighting spirit alive. Now they rose up in full strength and lit our enthusiasm again. There was a new spring in our step, our bearing was more upright and we made use of our weapons with 'exultant rage'. Once again we sang during troop movements and 'hurrahed' while storming forth in counter-attacks. The men fought with feverish eagerness. All of us were convinced that the Red Army would soon meet a withering defeat.

# 10

# 'Berlin bleibt Deutsch!'

The forces from the east did not take any notice of our reborn fighting spirit! They just kept on moving forward in the same inexhaustible stream as before. They pressed us implacably back, closer and closer to Berlin. The forest belt grew thinner, and gradually gave way to smaller suburbs with grocery shops, newsstands, post offices, cinemas and gardens. Violent engagements raged around and through these residential suburbs that now were ruined without mercy. There was hardly any reason for us to evade and spare them for an enemy who only brought devastation and mass murder with him. That was why we clung tight, as long as possible, in every small village, until the Bolsheviks had reached the flank or even had come behind us. Then we had to be quick and fight our way out. Several times every day we fought our way out of real death-traps in this manner. Every time, some of us were left there, having fallen into the trap.

The residential suburbs were our base, where we tried to hold out as long as possible in order to give time for the defence further back to get organised. But in between, the struggle went on as violently, if not even faster, out in terrain that varied between dense forests and open fields.

The day before we reached the limits of Greater Berlin, it could have been about 21 April, my platoon with the half-tracks was sent forward. We had to act as support to infantry soldiers of the *Wehrmacht* out in the open, who tried to delay Ivan. Our comrades were well dug-in facing the edge of the wood, out of which the hollering brown-yellow masses attacked, time after time. Here we suddenly and unexpectedly had to deal with Bolshevik infantry who had no proper artillery or tank support. Under such circumstances their losses were sure to be heavy, but that did not bother their commanders who just sent forth their people, totally without mercy.

As our mortars went into action behind a rise in the terrain, their loss of men increased even more. We let them come out some distance on to the field, then the rounds exploded over them with annihilating effect. They did not knock down just one or two men, but five or six fell in the grass or tried, bleeding, to drag themselves back after each impact. Then the Russians turned round and fled, as they thought, to the protecting edge of the wood. But they were met there by the same rain of steel, now even more effective because the rounds exploded against the tree trunks and so the shrapnel was given even more spread. Out in the field, in front of our positions, the number of fallen Russians increased. They were no longer lying one here and one there, but in tight groups. Our own men over there became enthusiastic at the platoon's precision of aim and were lying hurrahing in their foxholes.

Our ammunition was finished and a half-track was sent back to the supply unit to get fresh rounds. As we, smoking, were waiting for new ammunition and the next Bolshevik attack, we suddenly heard an un-mistakable clatter and the dull drone of tanks! Now our position was fin-ished! The German commander there obviously had the same opinion, because the infantry retreated, past us. But three men stayed in their po-sitions, volunteers with *Panzerfäuste*.

For us there was nothing else to do but to drive back. We could not resist though, driving up behind a group of trees and from there watch-ing the final outcome in the field. Between the sparse trunks we had a good view. The thunder of engines grew and came ever closer. There, at the edge of the forest, the treetops floated to and fro, as if a violent storm raged or a giant advanced. With creaking from the broken trunks, a huge armoured giant pressed down the last impeding trees and rolled out into the field. Close to it, one on each side, two others heaved their way for-ward and in their tracks two more followed. Firing at the retreating in-fantry they drove out into the field.

In the foxholes over there, three small human beings lay crouching, with their hands clenched hard around their *Panzerfäuste*, with thump-ing hearts listening to the ever louder thunder from the tank engines. Man against machine! Now the whole ground over there was trembling from the enormous weight of the giants. Rigid with excitement we stared out. There could not be 50 metres between them. They had no nerves, those three. The tanks maintained very small distances between each other, 10–12 metres perhaps, as they rolled forward. They had seen our infantry retreating and hardly thought that death could be waiting for them in the abandoned positions. Soon they were quite close to the three, still shooting at the retreating infantry, and taking no notice of the foxholes. My cigarette burned, unnoticed, between my fingers that were shaking with excitement.

For God's sake get up, now, before it is too late! The tanks had driven into a perfect position for the three comrades in the holes. The small gaps between them became their destruction. When the first tank had come to a distance of 10 metres, three heads and *Panzerfäuste* came up like lightning, three short bangs, fire shot out of the *Panzerfäuste* and three tanks were hit. Two of them were burning. One of them exploded almost immediately. The third rotated round and round on its damaged tracks. The heads disappeared quickly with the empty tubes and came up again with three new *Panzerfäuste*. Before it had time to withdraw from the *Panzerfäuste's* short range of fire, the rotating tank received its death-blow and at the same time the two remaining were penetrated by annihilating tank mines.

Five heavy tanks were burning out on the field, destroyed by three unknown infantry soldiers who now rushed up from the holes and in a zigzag ran back over the field to get away from the advancing Russian infantry. The bullets whistled around them and scratched up the earth around their feet. But before we rushed off to rejoin the company and avoid being surrounded, we could see our comrades disappear, unhurt, down into a dip in the ground.

The sun had been shining from a clear sky all morning. It was the hottest day of the whole spring so far. Summer was coming. In the gardens of the residential suburbs the fruit trees were blazing in the most wonderful blossom. Sprouting little buds had broken their covers and burst into fresh, light green leaves. How nice, just for an hour, to be allowed to forget the war, to forget the noise, to breathe the smells of nature, of fresh foliage and flowers, and to appreciate the coming of new life! But we could not take the peace and quiet for granted. Bloody events pushed us and chased us, from position to position. There was hardly time to take a few drags on a cigarette between the fights.

In the afternoon the company was ordered to dismount and go into action on foot. The drivers took the half-tracks back under cover from fighter planes. Under the command of Schwarck we went forward along the road that was to be blocked against the enemy tanks. Two other companies had the task of taking up frontal positions parallel to the road. To the left of the road, there was a belt of trees. We were given our positions, to keep the flank free. We had three machine-guns and a 7.5cm anti-tank gun as well as our usual small arms. We had a perfect shooting range against the open terrain, which separated us from the next belt of forest.

Tunics and shirts were taken off at once, and we started digging among tree-roots and stones. Thinking back, it is irresistible to make an amused comparison with the exercises in digging positions during the military training back home in Sweden. How idyllic that was! No exaggerated hurry, no unnecessary sweat, calmly and leisurely and with very little seriousness, the spades were turned. Who thought of the vitally important meaning of the ability to dig in rapidly? That ability, in war, meant as much for your life as handling your weapon the right way. Hundreds of thousands of lives had been wasted in this war, just because of laziness, and unwillingness to dig like moles.

But we, who now began to dig down in the stony ground of this forest belt, had seen enough of the war to know the meaning of the protection. Because of that we worked furiously, prized up stones, cut tree-roots and threw up earth with feverish speed. Our backs were bent like drawn bows, sinews and muscles were strained, sweat poured from our foreheads and flowed in streams down our naked backs. And you did not jeopardise your life for a smoke. The centimetres into the ground that you would lose could cost more than the taste of a cigarette.

The sun was blazing without mercy, and our throats ached from thirst. The Bolsheviks could turn up any moment. The sounds of battle were heard from all directions beyond the forest, and we redoubled our efforts to get deeper down. The blood pounded in the temples and the arm muscles quivered from the exertion.

Suddenly someone close to me 'hushed' and pointed at the edge of the forest on the other side. Everyone threw down the tools, put helmets on heads and jumped down into the holes with their weapons. Men came running fast over the field towards us. Our hands clutched the weapons harder and our eyes were screwed up, cool and calm, at the approaching soldiers. They were our *Fallschirmjäger!* Their characteristic helmets, that just in time told us their identity, saved them from being cut down by our machine-guns.

There were about 70 men, who came at top speed towards us. As they came closer, we stepped up from the holes. They were startled as they saw half-naked troops with submachine-guns in their hands, but Schwarck shouted to them. He called for their commander, a *Feldwebel* with the Knight's Cross, the Narvik shield and the *Kreta* cuffband, and let him give an overview of the situation over there. They had just been thrown out of their positions in the forest belt in front of us, but had only faced infantry. They had run out of ammunition, and then they had withdrawn. Their company commander had been killed, as well as the two men who had tried to bring back his body.

Schwarck decided that we should make a counter-attack. Since he had taken command over the *Fallschirmjäger*, we were a full company of more than a hundred men, just like in the old days. The newcomers got ammunition from our supply and then the entire force swarmed out into a firing line. I ran in the middle, beside Schwarck. Not a shot came as we crossed the field. In the forest belt it still remained peaceful, but as we came out in the open field again, it broke loose. Down! Schwarck turned panting to me "Shout like hell, as we rush up. The lads are almost finished, but we'll get them going if we shout altogether."

"Forward!" Schwarck shouted and I rushed up after him with a wild and husky "Hurrah!"

It was hard, because I was as tired and weary as the others, but it worked and the cry spread and echoed all over the narrow field, as we ran towards the violent infantry fire. As much as it stimulated us, it demoralised the enemy and in a flash we were over them. Like frightened rabbits they jumped out of their holes to get away, but our bursts reached their targets, no matter how they turned and twisted among the trees. We advanced and re-took some hundreds of metres as a defence sector for the *Fallschirmjäger*.

We promptly established a new defence of the contested forest belt. Ivan would not wait long before coming back. Schwarck, the *Feldwebel* and I went around and supervised the preparations. As I got furthest out on the right flank, it flashed into my mind that Schwarck had forgotten to connect with the companies by the road. In his eagerness to achieve a clever counter-attack, he had not thought of this important detail. Our position was unsupported.

By that time he was with the *Feldwebel*, away on the other flank, some hundreds of metres distant. It could be a matter of minutes. The last days' fights had brought so many sudden surprises and unexpected changes of situation that you had to be prepared for anything. A thundering clamour came suddenly from the blocking position by the road, where most likely Russian tanks were involved. I did not waste time running over to Schwarck to inform him, but sent a man to report that with three men, I had gone to take up the connection again.

We ran over the fields and through the forest for all we were worth. Now the sound of gunfire could clearly be heard from a group of villas that I knew were within the blocking position. From there came the typical dull, muffled 'crack' of tank guns. My fears grew. They were confirmed as we came out of the edge of the forest and could see the road in front of us.

There, the last men of the two companies ran for their lives onto the road. Several were lying there already. One of the fleeing, with one trouser-leg ripped open and flapping, waved excitedly at us, that we should run backwards. It was his last deed in life. The next moment he disappeared in the explosion of a shell from the Stalin tank that with mounted infantry had just appeared from a bend about 100 metres from us. The men at the left rear anti-tank gun managed to shoot away some of the infantry from the tank, before they were torn to pieces by a shell from the giant tank.

We turned around at once. Now it was really only a matter of seconds! The whole would be lost if the Bolsheviks in front of us and behind us managed to make contact and realise our situation before we had had the time to withdraw from the trap. We had to get further back before they 'squeezed the pincers' around us. Like hunted hares we leapt away over the fields, through the forest, to the company. There they had just begun to get new combat contact with Ivan again. Short bursts of fire whirled in among the trees at the forest edge on the other side, where the attacking enemy lay. In an instant I had Schwarck informed about the situation. He cursed wildly as we had to abandon the position without getting the chance to give the Bolsheviks a new fight. But there was nothing else to do than order the company out of there immediately.

To fool the Bolsheviks the machine-guns first fired continuously towards the edge of the forest, while the rest of our men withdrew. Then, the machine-guns were pulled out of the trenches, and brought into the forest. All the SS-men and *Fallschirmjäger*, at full speed, ran up hill and down dale. We remained in the narrow forest, and ran close to, but parallel with the road. We dared not get too close to the road. The Bolsheviks had most likely advanced a long way with their tanks. We ran about two kilometres with the sweat dripping. All the time, with a hammering heart, I thanked my lucky star that had brought not only myself, but also the entire company out of a terrible situation.

Eventually we turned up beside a road leading into a residential suburb, and there met comrades from our *Aufklärungs Abteilung*. They were the survivors of the two companies that, along with us, had tried to hold the blocking position. *Sturmbannführer* Saalbach was there, giving orders about the preparations for defence of the village. For the first time in a long time we now met some civilians, who intended to stay to await the arrival of the Red Army.

One of them was a fat red-faced grocer, whose acquaintance we made, as I along with Erich Lindenau and Kraus intended to enter the shop, to take in stores. We were hungry as hunters and had not had much other than haversack rations for the previous few days. He showed up at the door: "You won't get anything here without money!"

We looked at each other in amazement. So far we had only experienced civilians who pressed food on us. Lindenau, who was not what you call small and skinny, stepped forward to the grocer, pushed forward his chin and fastened his eyes on him:

"How dare you, old man! We are risking our lives for you! You should be glad that we are not Bolsheviks. They could cost you your life."

"Move over fatso!" Lindenau shouted, and pushed his submachine-gun into the man's belly.

The man went from red to quite green in the face and retreated, shaking. We pushed him aside and helped ourselves behind the counter, to sausage, butter and a loaf of bread. As we were standing there eating we threw one or two contemptuous glances at the trembling owner. Then the door was opened and the commander himself, *Sturmbannführer* Saalbach, entered. He saluted with a thundering "Heil Hitler!" and ordered a bottle of beer. We were already so at home in the shop, that it was natural for me to pass a bottle to him over the counter, before the nonplussed grocer had even moved a finger.

"It was nice of you to help my boys to food," the commander said, with a friendly smile on his dusty face, and handed over a bill, with the words "Keep the change!"

Cringing, bowing and repulsively smiling, the impudent shopkeeper opened the door for our commander, called him "*Oberst*" and croaked an ingratiating "Heil Hitler."

We put the remaining bread and sausages in our bags, jumped over the counter and headed for the door, without looking at the man. In the door Lindenau turned round, picked out a nice white visiting-card from his well worn wallet, and gave it to him.

"When the Russians are back over the mountains, you or you heirs can send me the invoice. Goodbye!"

He put a foot behind the grocer and gave him a push in the stomach so that he fell to the floor with a bump, went out and closed the door with a crash that broke the door-window into a thousand pieces.

The other civilians had disappeared and looked for safety in the shelters, as anti-tank guns and our light half-tracks were driven into position. Now the village really had that complete look of the frontline. Only the ruins were missing! The houses were undamaged and tidy, but that would soon change.

The three of us had orders to advance and observe, so that we could give notice when Ivan was coming. It seemed they had been delayed in some way, otherwise they would have been there already. In a ditch, in the shadows from some oaks, we found a perfect place. It was a short way from the road out of the village, but still it was bordered by numerous, very nice family houses, away towards the direction of the enemy. We lay chattering about everything, especially about the shabby fellow in the shop, while we chewed his sausages and bread, and kept a sharp eye on the road. It was nice to be lying that way in peace and quiet for a while, and enjoying the warmth of the spring. There was rumbling, and crashing in the surroundings, but right there it was calm and pleasant.

Kraus was looking hard at the bend in the road about 400 metres from us. He blinked his eyes and looked again.

"What idiot is coming here on a bicycle?" he said.

All three of us stared in that direction, speechless with amazement. Someone was actually cycling along all by himself, heedless, with no thought that the road, any second, could be under artillery or machine-gun fire. The bicycle wobbled from one side of the road to the other. Either the man was a beginner or he was drunk, most likely the latter, as he seemed to ignore the danger. It was too grotesque! A Sunday cyclist in no-man's-land! He must be both drunk and crazy!

It was an Ivan! When he was only 60–70 metres away from us, we could clearly see him. No wonder he was cycling so badly. It was probably the first time he had sat on a bicycle. In Soviet Russia only the Stachanov heroes could afford such luxury. He swayed along on his lady's bike in the sun, with his submachine-gun on his back and a dispatch-case at his side. With pleasure he enjoyed the sight of the nice houses and the well-kept gardens, not seen at home in Russia It was a shame to destroy the idyll, but that dispatch-case interested us. It might contain important papers.

So a life was finished, to save others. A poor Russian, like most of his fellow countrymen, harmless and kind when not incited to war by despots. With the mild nick-name of *Batjuschka* – little father – he was brutally interrupted on his life's first bicycle tour, that had taken him the wrong way in among the feared *Germanskij*. Riddled with bullets from a submachine-gun he tumbled over the bike. A figure turned up on the road in a flash, pulled the strap of the dispatch-case over his slack, dead arm and disappeared again. Fresh, young blood flowed over the asphalt.

Kraus ran back with the Russian dispatch-case, to give it to the company commander, to be forwarded to the Divisional staff. Before he had time to return to us, the Bolsheviks launched their attack against the village. It came from the south, on the flank. Now it was safer for the two of us to get back to the company before we were cut off. We threw ourselves over the road, down into the ditch on the other side, where we were better protected from the shooting, which now started to spread in our direction, too. Then we ran along the ditch, back into the village, where the fighting had already started. We defended ourselves stubbornly, but in the long run we could not hold the position against their tanks and artillery and, despite heavy losses, more of their advancing storm-troops. Struggling from house to house, in highly dangerous steeplechases, through open gardens, and turning around the corners of the houses to riddle the Red Army soldiers with some final bursts, we retreated to the north-west where the forest once again hid our small unit. The Stalin tanks could drive a bit further westwards on the highway.

Orders came that we must, at all costs, recapture the village and close the road again. Three King Tigers came, as much needed support. If we had not had them, it was likely that the counter-attack would not have started. We had come close to being physically and mentally finished.

The expectation of being able to stop the Red Army in front of Berlin, and of having the co-operation of the western enemies, had faded. In fact we were already standing just outside Berlin, and could see yellow and blue-red trains of the metropolitan railway, standing there and being shot to pieces on demolished embankments. Time after time we saw railway-stations with names that are associated with Berlin. Over and over again we saw signs for *Commerz-Bank, Lokal-Anzeiger* and *Berliner Morgenpost.* This was all extremely depressing. From more and more gable walls the words *Berlin bleibt Deutsch!* stared down on us. But now we began to ask ourselves with despair in our hearts "Will Berlin really remain German?" The last hope was now with *Obergruppenführer* Steiner and his northern army which, we were told, was on its way to our rescue.

In the twilight we advanced towards the small residential suburb, now on fire. Before the Bolsheviks had time to organise an efficient resistance, we were over them with new-born, furious, attacking energy, which the presence of the King Tigers had given us. With murderous determination we let the weapons play among the surprised Russians. They had felt secure for the night, and therefore had let the vodka flow. They fell in their drunkenness, and more than one enemy embraced his bottle in death. Those who managed to escape out into the darkness were easily picked off. Most were hit by a burst of gunfire or a hand grenade, when they showed up briefly as black shadows against the light from a burning house. We had recaptured the suburb.

Together with Lindenau, I happened to pass the grocery store. Over the iron fence, a broad, formless body was hanging. It was the grocer. The Bolsheviks had nailed him on the poles and tied his hands.

"I saved some money there," Lindenau whispered hoarsely.

I turned away and vomited. Of the remaining civilians all but one were found dead.

The only survivor was a 40 year old woman fatally wounded by one of our shells. She had been in the midst of a crowd of Red soldiers, who had begun to let loose their animal instincts on her. Why on earth had she stayed behind when most civilians had fled? She had had her husband reported as 'missing in action' at Stalingrad and had figured out that by staying behind she would, once behind the Red Army lines, sooner get in touch with him if he were still alive as POW. Now she lay there dying - the best that could happen to her instead of dragging herself through a life ruined by mass rape, slowly consumed by Siberian syphilis.

We quickly organised our defence. After a short while, a smaller column of trucks, full of unsuspecting Russians, came driving from the east. We let the cars through, and let them drive far in on the main street. Then, for several minutes our machine-guns and machine-pistols rattled against the cars. They swerved and skidded, crashed into house walls and fences, and overturned. We kept on firing until every movement in the chaos ceased, and the last cry of pain died out. With *Panzerfäuste* three Stalin tanks were knocked out the same way before the Bolsheviks became aware of the situation. During the night we had to defend ourselves almost uninterruptedly against their attacks, but now lacking the support from the Tiger tanks, we had to withdraw.

During the early hours of the morning orders came that our task was completed. Towards the north-west, for the hundredth time, we fought our way out of a Russian encirclement. Some comrades remained lying on the ground in the bursts of fire, but most of us escaped.

# 11

# From House to House

G*ross-Berlin* it said on a big yellow road sign that we passed as, in continuous fighting, we moved ever further westward that morning. It was a couple of days after 20 April, Hitler's birthday. We had left behind the wide belt of burning residential suburbs. Big factory blocks towered in front of us, and beyond them we could discern the sea of residential blocks of the giant city. A blue-grey haze lay like a veil over millions of inhabitants. It smothered everything with the dark smoke of vast conflagrations.

The western allies of Bolshevism were spreading even more destruction with their bomber armadas over the already badly damaged city. They had started the last great offensive, which would now go on nonstop until the day of surrender. We heard the thunder of bomb explosions in the centre of the city. We saw Flying Fortresses, in huge formations, making high-level sweeps across a sky that was speckled with small clouds from bursting anti-aircraft shells. Around the bomber formations, patterns in circles, curves, and lines, were woven by the vapour trails from the German fighters. The air combats were continuous.

From Küstrin and onwards we had experienced only the prelude so far. Now the real battle of Berlin began! The final struggle against the giants in east and west, the 'Twilight of the Gods', had reached its peak and passed into its last phase. We found positions, already prepared, that the civilian population had dug and built ever since the Russian breakthrough on the Vistula at the turn of the year.

At important road junctions the blockades against Russian tanks were standing ready to be dragged into positions with tractors or tanks. There were trams, filled with paving stones, and big freight wagons with well-known names such as *Knauer, Berliner Rollgesellschaft, Schmeling* and others. Small foxholes, which had been dug in on almost every street crossing, were mostly already manned by some *Volkssturm* men armed with a couple of *Panzerfäuste*. Everywhere *Volkssturm* soldiers could be seen, most of them with just a helmet and a badge as identification.

Among them, were lots of young boys from the *Hitlerjugend*, aged between eight and twelve or thirteen years. After a mercilessly cruel war of bombs they were just as hardened as old frontline veterans. In the middle of the worst bombardments they showed a confidence and a balance of mind that scared us. We thought that these boys should be playing harmlessly in the schoolyard. As the enemy became visible or could be located by his firing, the faces of these small boys assumed the same grim, hard resolute look as those of hardened veterans.

Added to the confidence in battle of these warlike children, came a rancorous frenzy and a boundless contempt of death, which we grownups could not muster. With the agility and speed of weasels they climbed and struggled their way into completely impossible positions, to knock out a Russian tank with a *Panzerfaust* or to finish off one or several advancing Red Army soldiers with a hand-grenade. There were quite a number of Russian tanks put out of action by small boys in their early teens during the battle of Berlin.

We were constantly forced back. Out in Karlshorst lay the great racecourse, one of the largest in the world. During peacetime, it attracted like a magnet, tens of thousands of horse-racing, enthusiastic Berliners and foreigners several times a week. We held this securely until 23 April. Then a violent battle developed around the circuit and its closest surroundings. On the green lawn in the middle, our mortars were brought into position, together with those of the neighbouring companies. The remaining platoons fought as infantry outside.

Whistling and howling Russian shells hit the stable-buildings and the platforms. Wooden benches and walls were splintered and whirled around in the air, and concrete walls were crushed. The artillery-fire grew into a rising crescendo from all sides. The great final bombardment of Berlin had begun. An impenetrable wall of gun-barrels closed, slowly but implacably, around the city. In the monotonously thumping thunder of the artillery and air bombs, the rattle of smallarms could only be heard at closer range. Amongst it all were the crashes of collapsing buildings.

The Bolsheviks had forced a barricade and broken through. Our own people were being chased over the track as we drove away. The Red Army soldiers were on our tail. Once again we were surrounded, and once again we managed to fight our way out.

Our next position of resistance became an enormous group of factories, crowned with the initials ASEA in giant letters. It became a fortress that temporarily held back the assault. The Russians losses were horrible, because we could fire at them from all possible angles, thanks to the location of the factory buildings. Then they put in heavy artillery. It sang and thundered all around and the blast-waves threw us, half conscious, to and fro between the walls. The defenders who were killed by collapsing walls, ceilings and iron-girders numbered more than those who got a direct hit, or were hit by splinters. It became unendurable to stay in this inferno. Whirling stone, scrap iron and bloody body-parts made the air impossible to breathe, filled as it was with limestone-dust and gunpowder gasses. Once more we fought our way out with Death just an inch behind us.

All day we fought our way back in this way. Surrounded over and over again, we struggled on through narrow passages and back streets. Often we passed right through the middle of the fighting-line of other units. We always got through but with steadily growing losses. Sometimes we could take the wounded with us, sometimes it was impossible, and they had to be left to await an enemy whose merciless brutality to SS men we knew only too well. The half-tracks had been sent back a long time before and we fought as infantry with our automatic weapons, *Panzerfäuste* and hand-grenades. We were hardly ever able to hold a position for more than an hour, then we were forced to run another race with Death, in the middle of Red Army soldiers.

It was unbelievable what masses they managed to throw at us. Constantly they advanced with their wild *urrää* yells, always supported by tanks. Many of their tanks were knocked out, but new ones constantly arrived. Despite that, their infantry were lying in bloody mounds in the streets and backyards, or were hanging out from smoke-blackened window-openings. But no weakening in their attacking strength could be noticed. Their losses in this struggle must have been horrifying to any army commander at all, except for a Soviet Marshal, but the reservoir did not dry up. (After the war it became official that 300,000 Red Army soldiers had died in the battle of Berlin)

There were still civilians everywhere. It was almost too late for them to try to escape the attacking Russians, who from the south had already advanced slightly west of Berlin and now were standing near Potsdam. Their assault had moved at such a breathtaking speed that the Berliners had had most escape-routes cut off before they even knew the worst.

Still, though, the stream of refugees went wide towards Potsdam and towards the north-west, near Nauen. But even if tens of thousands, or hundreds of thousands of people managed to escape from the encirclement, there were still millions left, who lacked the possibility of getting out. Public transport was at a standstill. With only a wheelbarrow, or a rickety bicycle those poor people did not manage to get far with their children and their most necessary belongings. First they had to force

themselves through the giant city's ruins, past blockages, over horse ca-
davers and human corpses that had already begun to pile up in the
streets.

The people who decided, or had to stay, went down into the shelters.
After all it was a life they had already got used to. They were cave-
dwellers in the 20th Century! Down there they grouped together, waiting anxiously, agonising, listening to the constantly approaching sounds
of battle. They felt the vibrations of the shell impacts and heard the
houses collapsing above them.

Tens of thousands of these terrified people were crushed under the
falling masses of stone. Or they were closed in from the outer world by a
collapse, to face an agonising death by thirst and starvation that first
drove them insane, before death came and relieved them. Those who
survived had to save every drop of water and every piece of bread as long
as possible. To run up from the cellar to bring water from the tap on the
nearest street corner was like running to meet Death. In this city there
hardly remained any silent spot. Merciless shells always seemed to find
an unfortunate victim.

We had been forced as far back as into Berlin-Lichtenberg. One afternoon we were suddenly pulled out of the battle and were sent urgently
southwards, down to Tempelhof and Mariendorf, where the Russians
had managed to make a dangerous penetration. It looked threatening for
the aerodrome in Tempelhof. The half-tracks were driven forward at a
raging speed along the burning Frankfurter Allee – Skalitzer Strasse –
Gitschiner Strasse – Belle-Alliance-Strasse and directly southwards.

Right in front of the gigantic administration buildings by
Tempelhof airport, at the Flughafen underground station, one year earlier on leave, I had managed to miraculously escape death, together with
a Swedish SS officer. It was during an American daylight attack, when a
heavy bomb penetrated the metre thick concrete roof of the railway station and killed many people. It was now a petrol depot on an open field
among barracks for Ukrainian workers. There the company stopped to
refuel. Among other comrades from the other platoons that I met during
this short pause was Ragnar 'the Giraffe' Johansson. During the hard
fights of the previous weeks we had not seen each other even once. He
was amazed to see me.

"Are you alive?" he asked, with audible doubt in his voice.

"Yes, as you can see."

"But the boys said that you got it at Küstrin," Ragge objected, obviously still not quite convinced. Then he smiled broadly, "Come, we must celebrate!"

He pulled me over to his half-track. From the inside he pulled a bottle, which he proudly showed off.

"Danziger Goldwasser! Good stuff. It's the company commander's, but we borrowed some. He can't take that much anyway," Ragge added with a tone which half excused, half intimated that we were doing a good deed by letting the commander be spared from drinking the whole bottle alone.

We took a big gulp each from the bottle of the noble drink, and then quietly and peacefully enjoyed a cigarette. It was the last time that I saw Ragge Johansson. A fine man and warrior, he was of a calibre that you do not find just anywhere. Ever since most of the Swedes in the Waffen-SS had gathered in our unit, he had been the connecting link. First as a motorcycle dispatch rider, then as the company commander's half-track driver, he had, thanks to his function in the company's staff, enjoyed greater opportunities for moving about than the rest of us. When the platoon was split up, he was the one who kept contact between the men, and he was a 'bringer of happiness,' who supplied us with rare newspapers and letters from back home.

As orders came to mount up, we just nodded, and cheered each other. We never thought that that could be the last time we saw each other. We had long since stopped worrying our heads about it. What would be, would be! But no oriental fatalism for us! Even if we had considered the possibility we still did not fall on each other, nor overdo our farewell. We knew each other so well! But a proper handshake would have been worthwhile and a simple but hearty "Thank you, Ragge! You were a strong soldier and a good comrade!" A high score for a good man!

The Bolsheviks had already reached Tempelhofer Hafen, 4-5 kilometres from the airport. In the residential suburbs of Lankwitz and Mariendorf we still held our positions, but in the open fields out to the east the Red Army soldiers had advanced like an avalanche and forced their way as far as the Teltow Canal. Right now the battle raged violently around the enormous group of printing and publishing company buildings at the south side of the canal, near the harbour. To prevent reinforcements getting through to our hard-pressed units on the other side of the canal the Bolsheviks laid a veritable barrage of bursting shells just over the blocks where we had to pass through.

The columns and masses of other troops that followed in our track were directed eastwards. Along Dorfstrasse and Germaniastrasse we drove down to Britz through a rain of shells. As we got there, we saw what was going to happen. The entire district was full of troops, infantry, artillery and several King Tigers. A heavy counter-attack was planned. Our entire Division was gathered.

As observer for a large number of mortars thrown together in a great hurry, I was lying with my field telephone in an advanced position in some ruins. It was quite peaceful there. Much worse was the sound of battle further away at the harbour. There everything was enveloped in an enormous column of smoke out of which fire sparked all the time. I could watch Russian tanks rolling forwards, with flashes repeatedly shooting out from their barrels. Between and behind the infantry soldiers crawled and ran. In the middle of it all, smoke and geyser of earth spouted up from German shell-bursts. The buildings out there were burning sky high and around them raged hard fighting. I lay crouched there, having seldom had the chance to get such an overview of a battle.

Our own counter-attack started. From our artillery in Britz, Lankwitz and Tempelhofer Feld a threatening thunder rose, that quickly grew to a roaring hurricane. Like a scythe the artillery fire cut into the Bolsheviks' rear areas and isolated their foremost tank and infantry units. Then came the moment for our mortars. Like a hail-shower their projectiles struck down among the advancing Russian masses of soldiers. The effect was increased by *Nebelwerfer* with their devastating explosive power. Regularly as clockwork the artillery fire thumped and thundered, and through its monotonous growling, howling *Nebelwerfer* projectiles cut their way forward to targets doomed to death. The area where the Bolsheviks had just pressed their way forward was transformed into a seething, smoking and fire-ridden maelstrom, where every second meant pain and death.

Behind me I heard engines growling. It was getting dark and in the fire-stained twilight our King Tigers, followed by infantry soldiers hardened by many assaults and close combats, rolled out of the ruins in Britz. They gushed forth in a powerful wave to crush what still remained of the Bolsheviks' bleeding spearhead. It was an immense and magnificent sight. For the last time I watched a tank battle. But it did not last long. Against our tanks the remaining Russian tanks could do little. It was like using slingshots against stone walls.

The gap was closed, but all night long Ivan threw forward new masses to retake the lost terrain and open the way towards the airport and the heart of the city. It was a terrible, bitter struggle without mercy. Like confetti-ribbons against the red-violet night sky the tracer bullets drew their flashing lines in all directions, spraying mercilessly against each target. Behind us a boundless sea of fire spread over burning Berlin, over which cruel monsters without interruption poured a murderous cargo to keep the giant fire alive.

It was incredible that there was anything left of the city. Since the last days of November 1943 it had hardly been granted any rest at all between bombing raids. The flames in the heart of the city stretched enormous arms towards the sky and produced heat that drove up a violent firestorm. The American armadas came in daytime. At night, the British practised 'area bombing', a ruthless invention by Air Marshal 'Bomber' Harris.

Hundreds of thousands of soldiers were now struggling in a wide ring around the city, with despair in their hearts against overwhelming odds. Towards them rushed an endless stream of shells from tens of thousands of gaping gun-barrels. (Supposedly, 40,000 Red Army artillery pieces hammered on Berlin). What we had managed to re-conquer in an evening was step by step taken away from us again the following day. At dawn, a pale sun rose over the smoking ruins of the great dying city and with some weak beams penetrated the heavy smoke clouds, down to the fire-blackened house walls with their empty gaping windows. Corpses lay in the streets and among the rubble.

Exhausted but still fighting defenders kept up the battle that had once again regained the previous day's character. From house to house, from cellar to cellar, and from street to street we were forced backwards. We had the enemy on our eastern flank by that time. Via Köpenick and Baumschulenweg he had advanced far westwards and reached the eastern outskirts of Britz. Our command had to rush reinforcements to that area to try to stop the assault. At the same time the pressure from the south-west increased. The situation had become extraordinarily dangerous.

Around noon on 25 April, the position could not be held any longer and we were forced to give up Britz to the Bolsheviks. To get over to Neukölln we had to cross the Teltow Canal. There was only a rather narrow bridge. The sounds of battle came ever closer, when the Division, as usual the last to retreat, withdrew down towards the canal. The small detachments that covered the retreat were hard-pressed. Things became nerve-racking for those waiting for the vehicles, gathered tightly on the street that ran along the canal bank. People from the entire Division were standing there, almost a thousand men, tightly packed. They were the remains of the old well-tried regiments Norge and Danmark, and other units of our Division. They waited anxiously, but it was not easy for the vehicles to force their way through the ruins.

At last they drove down towards the canal street and the crossing could begin. At that moment a desperate cry was heard from the rear: "Two Stalin tanks have broken through!"

The tank panic hit everyone. Hundreds of SS men, who for years had faced death innumerable times without loosing their heads, were caught by wild panic. They fled rashly, trying to escape up on the half-tracks. The companies behind pressed on and everything was squeezed to a compact mass. Into this mountain of human beings the shells and machine-gun bursts came flying from the two Russian tanks that had forced their way down the street. In front of me and behind me, to the right and to the left, bleeding and screaming soldiers fell to the ground.

What was left of the platoon I took with me to our half-tracks, which luckily were standing right at the front. As we got the vehicles started, hundreds of soldiers gathered around us desperately trying to climb up. The machine-gun fire and shell-splinters swept many of them away and the armoured sides of the half-tracks were turned red by their blood. As we moved down towards the bridge I saw that the fuse to the explosive charge under the bridge was already lit. In the panic someone had lit it too early. It squirted and sputtered from the fuse to the four rocket shells that were to blow the bridge into the air before the Bolsheviks could manage to get over. But how should we manage?

Behind us a volley from a Stalin organ hit the panic-stricken crowd with gruesome results. The men in the half-tracks did not know anything about the burning fuse under the bridge. They were already frightened enough. I stood with shaking knees while our vehicle slowly, slowly pressed its way over the bridge with the stream of fleeing men. Cold sweat came out on my forehead. Finally we were on the other side! Almost at the same moment as the half-track rolled off the bridge, the charge under the bridge exploded.

In the direction of Hermannstrasse the crew of an 88mm gun worked desperately to get the weapon in position, and to take the two Russian tanks under fire. Before they were ready, a new salvo from a Stalin organ came, hitting the north side of the canal and tearing to pieces the artillerymen.

What had happened to the other vehicles of my platoon? It was impossible to get a clear view of the situation on the other side. The iron construction of the bridge hung in the way and thick dust-clouds covered my sight. Had any of the half-tracks got up on the bridge as it was blown up or had the men jumped into the water? On the bridge, I had at a glance noticed that the remaining men started to jump into the water to swim over.

Filled with concern for the fate of our comrades, we drove along Hermannstrasse northwards. The gathering-point was U-Bahn Stadtmitte, where our Division Nordland's new command post was to be set up. For about an hour we zigzagged hither and thither on almost impassable streets. On a house wall we for the first time saw in hastily painted letters *SS-Verräter – Kriegsverlängerer!* ('SS traitors and extenders of war!') German communists had been at work. Was this the way it would be? Would they start to emerge from now on? Perhaps the civilian population's morale, which so far had stood up well under all the hard tests of the bombing war, had started to give way? Still we were saluted with "Heil Hitler!" when we sometimes stopped on a street to ask some water-carrying civilian the way to Stadtmitte. But perhaps it was only because of fear of the 'death's-head' soldiers that they saluted that way. Were we going to be forced to fight an inner enemy, too?

We had hardly completed this thought when right in the middle of Hermannplatz we had bursts of bullets sweep over the half-track from a roof. There, German communists with red armbands were lying shooting, with machine-guns that they had stolen from the *Volkssturm's* stocks. Soldiers from another SS unit came running, rushed up into a building on the other side of the square and put the roof over there under fire with their machine-guns, while some other men ran into the Communist house and set the upper floors on fire. Then they waited down by the front door, to see if the commies up there would prefer to die in the fire or try to get out, just to be caught and hanged from the nearest lamppost.

We watched other depressing signs of disorganisation on our roving way to Stadtmitte. Numerous *Wehrmacht* soldiers were standing loitering, weapon-less, in doorways. As they caught sight of our half-track, they quickly stepped back into the dusk. The respect the *Wehrmacht* had for the Waffen-SS was without limit. How many times out at the front, had we been sent into action to get them out of trouble, trouble that only the SS could solve? We also met *Wehrmacht* soldiers who, helplessly drunk, staggered around in the streets, without caring about the howling shells or air bombs. On the opposite side of the street an old man and some women were just tearing large pieces from a swollen dead horse. A whistling shell approached. They threw themselves to the ground behind the horse for a moment, awaited the impact, stood up again and continued with bloody hands to tear, scratch and cut in the cadaver.

At last we reached Stadtmitte. There was not a single undamaged house along the entire Leipziger Strasse, one of the most famous streets in the world. Here, illuminated advertisements of all colours used to shine. Expensive luxuries in world famous companies' magnificent shop-windows used to tempt the eyes of the strolling elite and the hurrying financiers and businessmen. Now, everything was grey and dull with remains of rusty iron constructions like gnawed skeletons poised over smoking piles of gravel and bricks.

Down in the underground station, privates and SS generals crowded together. I managed to find an *Untersturmführer* from my division, who gave me orders to carry on with the half-track to Grunewald, where the supply unit was, and to await orders there. As fast as possible we drove westwards. We crossed the totally devastated Potsdamer Platz, the torn heart of Berlin, and the Tiergarten Strasse, that now with its naked, splintered and fallen oaks looked more like a fossilised forest. We went up the Kurfürstendamm. In pre-war days its boulevard cafés had drawn people from all over the world to stroll along its elegant pavements, past luxury shops, and nightclubs known for their beautiful women. All had been swept away by the war's brutal fist. Then we went on through Halensee out to Hundekehle in Grunewald. There, in the forest round the lake, we found the supply unit.

We arrived at twilight and not until evening the next day had we moved on to reconnect with our struggling comrades down in Neukölln. The fact was that I had been kept behind to gather people from mortar platoons of regiments that no longer existed, except on paper. With four half-tracks and 20 men we could drive into the city. Among them were my reliable veterans Kraus, Leisegang and Lindenau, who had managed to swim over the Teltow Canal the day before and during the night had found their way to the supply unit.

All that was left of the company was in action some streets south of Hermannplatz. We drove in on a side street to Hermannstrasse with our half-tracks and I went down into the cellar where Schwarz had his 'company staff' - just a signalman - to get my instructions. Schwarz was sitting on a sugar-box and studied a map of Neukölln in the light from a storm-lamp. His face was bright red. On another box in front of him, he had a bottle of Danziger Goldwasser. It was almost empty. Schwarz was drunk.

With an unsteady finger he pointed out a street crossing to me: "Here you take position with the mortars. Keep Hermannstrasse south of Steinmetzstrasse and this park in Rixdorf under fire."

"Yes, but it's impossible to be out there. Ivan holds the further part of Hermannstrasse and can shoot directly at us."

"Don't you come here refusing orders! I'm in charge now!" Schwarz sounded and looked murderous.

"OK, but come on out yourself, damn it, and take a look!"

He slouched after me up the stairs and out on to the half-dark street, where the shadows of the ruins fluttered irregularly in the light from the fires. Just as we reached the corner to Hermannstrasse, a shell whistled past us and with a boom tore up the asphalt about 20 metres from us. Quickly we pulled our noses back and Schwarz changed his opinion about the suitability of a mortar position on Hermannstrasse. We had to remain on our side street with the mortars mounted on the half-tracks. Schwarz took Walther Leisegang as orderly and returned to the cellar.

To prevent the muzzle-flashes from the mortars from being seen from the air, we now fired in the semi-darkness with *Salzvorladung*, a wadding containing salt that dampened the muzzle-flash. The telephone which connected us with our observer over there was handled by Erich Lindenau down in the cellar, where worried and excited civilians sat pressed against the walls and in the corners.

Up in the sky a familiar rattling engine noise came from a Russian reconnaissance aircraft. It was of the type that the soldier's humour had given the name 'Iron Gustav' or 'Coffee-grinder.' The first name was because of this aircraft's custom, like an inspecting Sergeant-major, of turning up anywhere, and slowly, flying back and forth, even in the most violent anti-aircraft fire. The other name, because of the typical motor hum that mostly sounded like an old coffee-grinder's creaking. It swept back and forth, at hardly 100 metres height, and searched and searched, maybe for us?

Together with Kraus I was on my way down to Lindenau, on what errand I do not remember any more. We had just put our feet on the first step to the cellar, when suddenly the entire gable collapsed over us. A violent air pressure tore our helmets off and we were half buried in gravel and lumber. Kraus got on his feet right away. There had been an explosion close behind, right among the vehicles! Kraus went down again under the pressure, but was up again at once, unhurt. I tried to crawl to my feet, but failed.

From the half-tracks on the street cries and groans were heard and the sound of exploding ammunition, and down in the cellar the women cried hysterically.

Damn! What could this mean? It was quite impossible to get to my feet. At last, Kraus took my arm and helped me. My uniform was torn to shreds, and grey from limestone dust. My nice soft officers' boots, that I had been so happy about, were completely ripped. Staggering, I managed to get down the half-demolished stair to Lindenau. It hurt a bit in my left thigh and I touched the leg with my hand. It got quite wet. It was blood. And now the burning pain came. I was wounded. There was a large, wide-open hole all the way through the thigh. Out there the mortar ammunition continued to explode. The cries got fewer and weaker.

"Look! I'm wounded," I said and showed Kraus and Lindenau my bloody hand.

They grabbed me around the waist and with my arms over their shoulders I hopped on one leg up the stairs, over the pile of stones in front of the entrance. Our half-tracks looked like scrap! They were burning, and the crews lay spread here and there. The entire platoon of about 20 men had been annihilated! Explosions still came from our ammunition supply. But the cries had stopped. Supported by my good comrades I limped along the house walls on Hermannstrasse and around the corner down to Schwarz's cellar. There I could lie down on the floor. Kraus and Lindenau pulled off my boots and trousers, while Schwarz and Walther Leisegang got a bottle of schnapps, out of which I took some swigs to get a little bit more alert. But despite that I felt quite weak and the blood was flowing steadily.

It was a large wound caused by bomb splinters from the 'Iron Gustav' that had sneaked around above our heads. I could have put my fingers in the wound. Walther put a cigarette between my lips and I lay there puffing, while Kraus made some sort of bandage, which very soon was soaked wet by my blood. The alcohol and the weakness put me into a pleasant lassitude. The tension was over, I thought, and it was nice to lie still like this and think of just about nothing. It took quite a while, until the men found a stretcher.

During that time the Russian artillery shot away half the house, and the building next to us collapsed completely, so that the civilians who had been sitting in its shelter had to hack their way out through the basement walls to our cellar. They ran hysterically hither and thither and cried out every time whistling from a bomb or shell was heard from outside. Indolently, I listened with half an ear to their noise. Our men tried to calm them down, but apparently they did not manage too well.

At last someone managed to find a stretcher. Kraus, Lindenau and Leisegang all came along and helped to carry me. It was not a peaceful or comfortable transport. Time after time shells came howling, so that they had to run into some doorway with me, where they heaved the stretcher around quite roughly. I was not the only one on my way to the first-aid station at Hermannplatz. Many wounded soldiers came, drawn on old damaged bicycles, on hand-carts, and in prams that almost gave way under their weight.

In a great storage-cellar on Hermannplatz I was laid on a table which was covered with blood. I got a couple of injections against tetanus and a friendly soul put a nice bandage on with quick, but gentle, fingers. The wounded were lying tightly packed all over the floor and the air was filled with cries, moans and groaning wheezes, that echoed against the vaulted ceiling. My men stayed until I was ready to be loaded into an ambulance. Then they approached the stretcher to say "goodbye" to me.

It was a tough moment. We had struggled together for a year, a long time in this war and had been the backbone of a strong platoon. All joy and all misery we had shared equally, and side by side gone through hell on the Eastern Front. Now I was finished with the war – at least for the time being - but what lay ahead for these three? Were they going to be killed now, in the final phase of the war, these magnificent men? There were no better mortar crewmen to be found. It was with such men that our platoon in Courland had managed to achieve what is not done every day in a war, to knock out a Russian tank with mortars. Their chance to get away alive was so exceedingly small and although they smiled at me, as they now shook my hands in farewell, I could see the fear of what was waiting for them shine out of their eyes. I was almost ashamed to leave them.

In an ambulance I was taken on a roving tour through the central parts of the city. We drove from hospital to hospital, but everywhere got the answer "Full!" Finally I was left temporarily in a hospital somewhere near Lützowplatz. I was told that I should be moved as soon as possible down to the big hospital in the Thomaskeller – one of Berlin's greatest beer-halls – not far from the Anhalter Bahnhof. As I was lying there waiting, I started to imagine what it might be like down there in the Thomaskeller. Of course there would be some thousand men lying in the enormous cellar. There would be the stench of blood and pus, the cacophony of moans from thousands of mouths day and night, dead and dying lying around between the white-tiled walls. No, it would be too much of a slaughterhouse! I could not stand the thought of lying there in Thomaskeller.

So I made my decision. I had to get away from there, before the transport would come to pick me up. Just next to where I was lying, was a bloody, wooden box that had been used to carry in the wounded. I broke loose a board from it to use as support. Then I stood up and staggered up the stairs and out on the street. The day was breaking through. I felt dizzy and weak, but started limping away. I did not have any target, but it struck my mind, that perhaps I could find shelter in the big anti-aircraft bunker up by the Zoo. The wound burned and thumped violently in my leg and I felt sick. Wherever I looked, there were dead bodies in the streets, almost all civilians. No one had the time to bury all these dead and it already started to smell awful. The streets were covered with remains of houses and burnt out vehicles and it cost me great efforts, using the board, to shuffle along.

Down on Keithstrasse I fainted. I woke up to find that a young girl was holding my head on her knees. Of course I thought I was dreaming, but a look at the surroundings convinced me that it was real. She helped me up on my sagging, unhurt leg and took me over a pile of stones and into the house where she was living. There her mother met me. They started cooking some food and put a bottle of wine on the table. They tried everything to cheer me up, telling me that the Russians had been pushed back from Grunewald, where they had broken in the day before, just after my platoon had left there. They also told me that *Obergruppenführer* Steiner was on his way to relieve Berlin with his northern army. Good old Felix Steiner! When I told them that I was Swedish, they became if possible, even more helpful. The girl said "But why don't you try to get to the Swedish Legation's bunker?"

I had not thought of that! But it was just nearby.

After having got my strength up with all that good food they had nearly forced me to eat, I set off, with the girl to help me. It was a good thing that she came along and supported me, otherwise I do not think that I could have managed to walk the kilometre alone. Up at the corner of Rauchstrasse and Friedrich-Wilheim-Strasse she said farewell and I limped the last few steps alone.

As I caught sight of the bunker in the legation garden I saw a group of people standing smoking outside its entrance. They were all dressed up, well combed and tidy. Obviously they were Swedes. Swedes have a certain ability to keep the external style even in the most fretful situations. To my shame I myself was an exception this time. Three weeks worth of bristles were growing wildly on my chin, and dirt gave me a Balkan-like swarthiness. My clothes consisted of a dusty steel helmet, an indescribably dirty and torn greatcoat, a thick layer of dirt on my naked legs, as I had left my trousers in the cellar on Hermannstrasse, and a pair of boots cut to pieces by splinters. This outfit was completed by a submachine-gun, dangling on my chest from a strap around my neck, an awe-inspiring parabellum stuck down in the belt and a pair of hand grenades sticking up from my boots. No wonder that the group stepped back a bit closer to the bunker entrance, as I came limping towards them. Amongst them was a 'fine' lady. How fine she was, I soon realised as she reacted to my probably quite disconcerting appearance. She stage-whispered to the now quite pale-faced gentlemen "Imagine that there are such Swedes!"

Later it came to my knowledge that her name was von Ungern-Sternberg, baroness. 'Noblesse oblige', so to say. Oh well! I did not let this ominous prelude scare me off, and put forward a discreet plea to be allowed down into the bunker and recover for a while. I showed the blood-drenched bandage and explained that I did not feel quite well and would appreciate an hour's sleep, as I had not slept much in the last few weeks. At that moment one of the gentlemen did not care about keeping his distance any more and bravely advanced a bit towards me. From what he said I realised that I was facing a first-class diplomat

I would have to put in a written application for permission to enter, but he let me understand that I, under the laws of war, could not enter the strictly neutral Swedish bunker. Obviously it had something to do with international law and so forth. As I did not want to get the company, and old Sweden, involved in such a horrible war crime, I slowly started to retreat from this piece of Swedish land. Then another gentleman turned up out of the bunker. He was given a quick briefing about the situation and called me back. He was the physician of the Legation.

"Come with me," he said and helped me down the stairs.

He led me to a bed, where I could stretch out, after having put the weapons aside.

He shuddered as he saw my wound. "Ugh!" he said, then smiled. He added "Well, how are we feeling today?"

It was just like 'Uncle Doctor' when you were a little boy in school. I was so happy I could have wept! He took care of me in the most touching way, took off the old blood-soaked bandage and applied a new nice Swedish bandage, material of pre-war quality. All the time he chatted with me about anything and everything, gave me cigarettes, and advised me to remain lying down and try to rest. But I was thinking about the people outside and that made me lose all desire for it. So I thanked him, gathered my weapons and limped away with my board.

I remembered that one of my Swedish comrades, *Untersturmführer* Gunnar Eklöf, an officer from our *Abteilung*, recently had had a command in Berlin, as the city became the front line. Perhaps he was to be found in his apartment at Gertraudenstrasse. I started to move in that direction, towards Wilmersdorf. There every street crossing was equipped with a tank barricade and it was difficult to get through. As I finally reached my destination, it was clear that the house was empty. On again.

Now I did not know what to do. From the lightly wounded who came walking past, I was told that the Red Army already had advanced to Fehrbelliner Platz. Close to where I was our own infantry had taken position and violent firing could be heard from there. The houses around me were on fire. The smoke, mixed with the stench from the dead bodies in the streets, turned into a disgusting smell. Irresolutely I limped out onto Kaiserallee. There everything suddenly went black for me and for the second time I lost consciousness.

I came to just as a motorbike stopped by my side. Two SS men jumped off and lifted me up into the sidecar. In a flying hurry they drove me down to Nikolsburger Platz and left me in a school that now served as hospital. I was helped into a big pillared hall, where the floor was tightly packed with wounded. The shelter and the lower floors were overflowing, and the upper floors were partly damaged by air bombs. Carefully climbing over the wounded I managed to advance to a bench and sat down next to a *Feldwebel* from the *Wehrmacht*.

He was a giant of a man. He wore the Knight's Cross round his neck and had his head covered with bandages. He had been shot in the head. Another wounded man told me that the *Feldwebel* was blind, half-paralysed and unconscious. He reclined, leaned moaning against the wall. Once his picture had been published in all German newspapers and he had been honoured as a hero. Now he was sitting there helpless. No one had time for him. The poor Red Cross nurses ran hurrying to and fro and had to take care of new wounded all the time. He had got his bandage and they could do no more for him. It was horrible to see this physically magnificent specimen, now a helpless wreck.

I cannot describe the night that followed, all the suffering I saw and all the piercing groaning I heard. Until next morning I remained sitting on the bench, smoking non-stop to calm my nerves, surrounded by mutilated, dying and dead. In all there were 1,300–1,400 suffering human beings.

In the morning, when the orderlies started to carry away the ones who had died during the night, I got a provisional bed. Before that I was laid upon an operating table, got a couple of injections and a new bandage. My closest neighbour became a NCO from the *Wehrmacht*. His name was Walther Heinau. He came from Upper Silesia, was about 20 years old, and had volunteered in 1942. He had lost a leg. Then he voluntarily served as an infantry soldier, with an artificial limb. Now he was lying there with the back of both his thighs shot away. He had got away from the Russians with his life by cycling, with the blood streaming heavily from his legs, to the nearest first-aid station. A magnificent boy! But now he was depressed. Up to the last minute he had wanted to believe in victory, but what was now to be expected? He expressed his despair with an Upper Silesian curse that he repeated all the time, 'Pironny!'

On 28 April we got proper camp-beds to lie in. The fighting had advanced closer to us and the building vibrated from the cannonades. Even more wounded were brought in, many just to die shortly after their arrival. Most of them were indescribably maimed. It became even more difficult to find food and drinking water. A proper care for the wounded was not realistic. But Heinau still had cigarettes, so the two of us managed pretty well.

On 29 April the struggle raged very close to us and we lay listening anxiously to the violent exchanges of fire. Any moment shells could come whistling in among us. We felt miserably small. Like other wounded SS men I started to remove my SS insignia. The pay-book and my Swedish passport I got rid of, too. The passport was as much a death sentence to me, in the eyes of the Bolsheviks, as the Waffen-SS pay-book, because the photo showed me in Finnish uniform and there was also a stamp regarding my participation as a volunteer in Finland in 1941.

During the night of 30 April the firing outside started to move away and then we knew that the Russians could be there at any moment. In the morning they came storming in, dirty, bad-smelling in a quite special, typical Red Army way, and with their submachine-guns up and ready. They started to snoop around everywhere, leering and sneering at the wounded, but otherwise they behaved correctly. Actually 'Berlin kaputt!' was their stock phrase.

Then they started to examine every man. They went from bed to bed, pointing the submachine-gun at the chest of the wounded and asked: "You SS man?" There were several hundred SS men lying there with their hearts in their mouths, but all of them had removed their SS insignia and denied stubbornly. After all, they wanted to stay alive. A small bow-legged, flat-nosed half-Mongolian approached me. "Du SS?" he hissed out and forced the gun barrel deep into the pit of my stomach. I protested that I was an ordinary *Wehrmacht* soldier. "Da, da du SS?" he repeated and in my panic I thought I saw that everybody's eyes were on me. Then I managed to achieve something that reminded him of a smile and shook my head. Then he gave up. I was drenched in a cold sweat, but could now breathe more easily.

The Bolsheviks immediately started a careful clearance of the upper floors. Bricks and mortar were heaved away and we were moved up. Then we also got drinking water and a thin coffee. Russian doctors came and helped care for the worst wounded. They started amputating, but without anaesthesia. I guess that about 90% of the amputated bled to death. I got a new bandage. And it was just in time, because the old one was stiff with dried blood and pus and stank terribly.

In the afternoon of 1 May, Red Army soldiers came and told us, laughing, that Hitler was dead. "Chitler kaputt! Chitler kaputt! Bärrlin kaputt! Garmanija kaputt!" they roared. Heinau wept silently.

# 12

# Towards Freedom!

As the sounds of battle died away in the ruins of the great destroyed city, an order came from the Russian commandant. All wounded, with Berlin as their home address, could return to their homes and all the other wounded were allowed to have visitors. We were not prisoners any more! But before anyone had time to leave, there were counter-orders. No one was allowed to leave the hospital! Some Berliners escaped despite that, with the consequence that guards were placed around the building. An officer arrived and explained, in broken German, that anyone who tried to escape would get 'a shot in the neck'.

My situation seemed hopeless. How could I get away? I wrote a letter to the Legation, and a German nurse with a pass smuggled it out. There was no answer. I began to get nervous. I was on my feet and could move around. Beds were needed for the more severely wounded. I had to help to bring out the dead. But first we had to pull off their hospital clothes and put their uniforms back on them. Between 50 and 75 men died there every day and I was never out of work.

That I came out of all this with my senses intact seems unbelievable today. We carried the dead down to the street and from there the Red Army soldiers removed the corpses. They threw them carelessly on lorries and drove away to a nearby mass grave in a park. At night I had horrible nightmares. One night when I was in the washroom, one of the other corpse-bearers came and fetched me.

"You have a visitor," he said.

By my bed a Red Cross nurse was sitting speaking with Heinau. It appeared she was a Swedish woman married to a German. She had heard that there was a Swede in the hospital. We talked over my situation, and she promised to visit the Legation to try to get a provisional passport for me. Furthermore we agreed to try to arrange a few luxuries for the coming Whitsun Eve. The Swedish nurse assured us that she could organise a bottle of wine and something to eat, more than our scanty rations.

The senior Russian doctor was very interested in me. It was so obvious that I got suspicious. He always had time for a chat and he would ask me about absolutely everything. This meant that I had to construct a completely new life, because I still, of course, insisted that I was an ordinary German *Wehrmacht* soldier. It was important to keep control over my tongue and many times I came close to letting out my secret. But thanks to his interest in me, I also had my wound cared for and my recovery was quick. He was a sympathetic man of the Western European sort and many times I wondered how he could fit in with his Bolshevik surroundings. It was hardly the right place for a man like him, who was humane and cultivated.

Whitsun Day came, but in a completely different way than I had expected. We were awakened just before six o'clock. Red Army soldiers came tramping into the halls, waking us up with loud shouts and shakings. Everyone who could stand on his feet had to leave his bed and change from hospital clothes to uniform. The hospital was to be evacuated. We were told that all the wounded were to be transported east, to an assembly camp for wounded prisoners of war.

There I was, without passport, without money, without any other clothes except my uniform. I was desperate. Thoughts just went around in my brain as I made my bed and got ready. One escape plan after another was born and died. It was just hopeless. How could I manage to disappear? All exits, even the halls, were guarded by Red Army soldiers with submachine-guns. This had to be the end. It just had to be that the Bolsheviks would check my uniform more closely in the next camp. They would see the traces of the SS insignia on the collar and sleeve, and I would be taken away to get a shot in the neck.

The guards hurried us. Time was short. We started to carry down the most badly wounded, on stretchers, to the long column of Russian lorries that would take us east. The second time I went down with a stretcher I met our nurse, who came, half running, with a big parcel under her arm.

"You must come with me up to the hall, at once," she said earnestly and hastily.

A comrade took my end of the stretcher and I limped along with her up the stairs as fast as I could. While we were walking, she explained the situation and told me what I had to do.

"Take this," she said and gave me a big envelope. "Here is also a suit and a pair of shoes."

I needed no further explanation but rushed into the washroom. As fast as I could I took off the uniform, tore open the parcel and put on a brand new sports suit, and a pair of 'as good as new' brown shoes. How had she managed to find these things in this devastated city, where such things had not been possible to find for the last few years? I had no time to think of that and instead I opened the envelope with fingers shaking with anxiety and excitement. Some ten Mark bills and a Swedish emergency passport were there. My heart, which all morning had stuck tight in my throat, slowly sank to its normal position and I could think and plan calmly and easily once more.

It was a new man from top to toe who now went out from the washroom. I had my pass in the breast pocket and with that as a weapon, I knew that I somehow should make it. I looked around for my fellow countrywoman to thank her. She was gone. I did not have time to try to find her, because the loading of the wounded was completed and everyone was ordered to mount up. The others on the platform stared, as I climbed up dressed in my elegant clothes.

The long column drove out from Nikolsburger Platz. In passing I registered the sight of one of our company's recce half-tracks, knocked out and burned out. Around it some twisted bodies of fallen comrades. So they had fought there too, during the last days. How was the situation for GP and the other men by now? Were any of them still alive? Once again I had to wonder at my fabulous luck. What now remained was for me to manage to get through. It had to be 'a piece of cake!'

It was not good for the morale in the column to be forced to make this trip through Berlin. Certainly the sounds of battle were not heard any more and the giant fires had died out. Perhaps it was just because of that that the impression was so terrible, so heart-breaking. During combat you were busy defending your own life. The dense smoke and fog had made it difficult to see. Because of that you didn't have a clear view of the destruction. Now it appeared so much clearer, and much sharper. Even though several days had passed since the end of the fighting, many corpses were still lying in the streets. Otherwise they were almost empty of people. An old man or old woman, or a woman with a couple of dirty and pale children could be seen crawling out of the ruins. The streets were in many cases full of knocked out tanks, guns, burned out cars and all sorts of scattered materials. All the time we passed well-armed enemy patrols. Most of the Red Army soldiers had typical Mongolian looks.

Ghengis Khan's descendants were masters over Berlin. They had already had time to put up signs with street names in Russian, and here and there we saw propaganda posters, with Stalin's picture in giant sizes. Motzstrasse – Bülowstrasse – Potsdamer Strasse – Leipziger Strasse – Alt-Stadt – Landsberger Strasse – Landsberger Allee – all were just heaps of bricks and mortar, or fire-blackened house fronts with empty window frames. There was nothing behind them. There was an unbelievable, indescribable devastation. Could this ever be a city again, the home of hu-man beings? Anyone who started to tidy up here would surely drown in the rubble.

Then at last we came out of the ghost city and into the suburbs. The column drove in between guards into a barbed wire enclosure and stopped in front of a big brick building that looked like a school. We were ordered to get down and lift out the stretcher cases. The building was already more than full. Because of that, the stretchers had to be placed on a lawn, where other lightly wounded prisoners were just set-ting up tents. Many German soldiers were lying all around. There could have been 3–4,000 men.

By a freak of fate I met one of the men from the 3rd Company. He came from a similar hospital in Schöneberg and could tell me that there had also been two American officers, volunteers from the Waffen-SS, and some Swedes from Leibstandarte SS 'Adolf Hitler,' whom the Ger-man doctors had refused to send out with the transport from there. Strangely enough they had managed to make their get away and so the Americans and the Swedes had 'got lost' in the confusion, before the transportation. Also he had found out that the same evening we were go-ing to be taken further east, first to Frankfurt-an-der-Oder. To be for-warded to - where?

I was not going to spend any more time in this place! I found out where the camp commandant had his office. It was in a villa a couple of hundred metres from the camp. One of the guards, all of whom were women, I managed to persuade to take me there, thanks to my pass which I waved under her nose. The commandant agreed to see me. So I drew myself up, stuck out my chest and marched in. It came as a well-memorised string: "I am a Swedish engineer studying in Berlin, unfortu-nately I was wounded during the battle, and brought out here by mis-take. I need to be set free immediately in order to go home," and so on.

The general waved away a cloud from his *papirossij*, peered closely at me and lounged about in the comfortable armchair of a quality that would be hard to find in the Soviet Union.

"Nitsjevo, nitsjevo."

He could do nothing. My pass did not impress him at all. I could turn to his colleague in Frankfurt, he advised me. Aha, I thought, that means that I can go on like this, getting the same answer, until I have reached the end station beyond the Urals.

Worried, I returned to the camp, with the murderous Soviet 'ama-zon's' gun-barrel pointing threateningly at my back. After a while I made a cheeky attempt to get out. I approached one of the guards at the entrance, showed her the passport and said that I had the right to pass.

"Nje ponimaju (I don't understand)," she said, stared grimly at me and pressed the submachine-gun into the firing position under her arm.

I backed off promptly. But I had not given up. I just had to wait for the right moment. In one of my jacket pockets I had found a packet of cigarettes that my thoughtful guardian angel had put there. Smoking, I rambled about near the exit.

Then came the changing of the guards. They were male Red Army soldiers this time. Suddenly, there was only one guard at the entrance, a boy with a kind, harmless face. I went to him, offered him a cigarette and started to mangle my Russian. They were good cigarettes and the words I spoke were nice, too, as far as he understood them. As soon as I judged the ground prepared enough, I took the passport out of my pocket, pointed at the stamp and said that I could go and visit the commandant, with whom I was already acquainted. The stamp did it! In the Red Army only divisional generals and higher commanders stamp orders and documents. He let me pass right away!

Slowly I strolled a bit towards the commandant's villa, but as I went out of sight of the guard, I took off on a side path. And now I got my legs working, with no pauses other than short stops to rest my bad leg, where the wound was still so large that I could get my whole thumb in it. I now walked 30–40 kilometres. First I walked through the suburbs, and then through half of Berlin.

My target was the Legation's bunker. On my way through the city I was stopped several times, but the pass-stamp saved me. The Berliners now started to show up more frequently, and although still frightened, they found their way along the streets. Each one who was stopped by a patrol was stripped bare of all their property, watches, rings, suitcases, glasses, in fact all loose objects.

Having reached Wilhelmplatz I stopped dead. On a gallows in front of the Reichs Chancellery a male corpse was hanging. I went closer. It looked like Goebbels! Although the Bolsheviks had crushed his nose and given the corpse a deep bayonet stab in the throat, it was impossible to be mistaken. Civilians who came walking turned their heads away as they passed the gallows. But Red Army soldiers stopped in groups, pointed at the hanging body, and laughed.

During my walk I noticed that the Red propaganda was working in another way, too. In front of every baker's store was a sign that said, 'Hitler took the bread from the worker. Stalin gives it back to him!' To the

German worker this was a ridiculous statement, as he under the National Socialist rule had been set free from the Weimar period of unemployment and poverty. He had finally been given the chance to build a better life, which in some essential parts even surpassed that of the Swedish worker. Now bread was sold for a few days without rationing, which had the consequence that stocks soon began to run short and the population began to starve.

In the evening I reached the Legation's bunker. Some women were standing outside, and they told me that the Swedes had left Berlin. I was permitted to enter the bunker, where the women, Swedish women married to Germans, piled up lots of delicacies whose existence I had almost forgotten, such as chocolate, real coffee, Danish bacon, and Camel cigarettes. Then I was picked up by another Swede. I was taken to an apartment at Budapeststrasse, where a number of my fellow countrymen and women lived, while waiting for the chance to get home.

For almost two weeks I stayed there, without going out in the street even once. There was no point in risking my life. No non-Soviet was absolutely safe and secure. Everywhere commandos from the Red Army popped up and snatched people away. Day and night you could hear how they were blowing up and shooting in the city. We preferred to sit inside and use up our stocks from the bunker.

Among those who were living there was a Swedish sailor. He had recently been released from a German concentration camp, where he had been sent because of having spread communist propaganda in some German harbour. He cursed and blamed the Germans, and every day and hour he expressed his wish that the Russians should exterminate the 'rabble.' Later, according to the Swedish press, he was put into a Russian concentration camp outside Moscow, where he probably lost the inclination for further Communist propaganda.

Gradually it became too trying to sit inside, especially as we were told that the GPU was in action. They had started to show up here and there in their hunt for 'patriots'. One day I could not stand it and went out to scout around. I trudged out on streets where I had never walked before. At a safe distance I was witness to how the GPU made a raid. They closed an entire block, forced many of the inhabitants on to trucks and took off towards unknown destinations.

Somewhere between Kaiserdamm and Kurfürstendamm, near Stuttgarter Platz, I stopped dead, dumbfounded! I had an experience that would usually only occur in a book. Who was standing there on a corner, looking at the ruins, if not my fellow countryman

*Untersturmführer* Eklof! The day before I was taken to the hospital, I had been looking for him at Gertraudenstrasse! The first thing he told me was that GP too, was alive. I jumped for joy!

We immediately went away to GP's hideout. He could not believe his eyes, as he suspiciously opened the door a few centimetres and saw me. It became quite a celebration party and while we were sitting there I was told his story of the last days' struggles. It was fantastic. Even if I have to leave out parts, I very much want to tell some of it.

On one of the last days he had again taken command of the 3rd Company. The new company commander had fallen. The Division was thrown first here, then there during the battle. He also confirmed that the company had been fighting near Nikolsburger Platz, where I had seen the knocked out half-track. That was the last day it was in action, at Friedrichstrasse. There his command half-track was knocked out and started to burn, close to the railway viaduct by the subway station. The crew jumped out of the vehicle, but all were killed except GP, and Ragnar Johansson 'II' who ran towards the viaduct. GP saw Ragge fall, as he ran. He rose again, fell once more, and remained lying still.

Alone, GP ran in under the viaduct. He happened to look up and caught sight of a Red Army soldier on an iron girder just ready to drop down a hand-grenade at him. He ran behind a projecting concrete wall and let the hand-grenade explode. Then he ran into a gateway, up the stairs and into an apartment. By chance he came upon a wallpaper-covered door, well hidden behind a chimney-stack, and crept through.

He had not been sitting there very long, before Ivans came tramping into the house and started hunting around. They crushed furniture, turned apartments upside down and soon found two other SS men, who had also been hiding in the same apartment. With his body in a cold sweat, GP heard the SS men shot, on the spot. But he managed to remain undiscovered. He stayed in his cubby-hole for two days and nights.

The third day he cautiously dared to come out from his hideout and sneaked down the stairs. In the dusky backyard he met an old woman, who assured him that the Red Army soldiers had not been seen since their first round-up. GP sighed with relief and went out the back way into a shop in the house. The owner promised to get him a set of civilian clothes. While GP was sitting there waiting, he happened to take a look out on the street. There was the old woman with three Red Army soldiers! Stumbling, he ran out, over the yard, up the stairs and into his hideout. Heavy steps on the stairs, male voices, rough, and the informer's, shrill, came closer.

The alarm bells rang for GP. The wallpaper-covered door was flung open, three submachine-guns pointed into the darkness and a harsh voice roared that he should come out. It was a shock and GP fumbled about to support himself. Then his hand grabbed something soft. It was cloth. He quickly realised that it was a military tunic. His officer's tunic of the Waffen-SS, with decorations, would betray him, so in furious speed he changed before he stepped out into the daylight. As he came out through the door his first glance was at his left tunic sleeve. There was not the SS insignia that he had feared. He was wearing a standard tunic for a corporal of the regular army. GP felt such a relief that he could have fainted. After that, like me, he was sent to a POW camp. How he managed to get out of there, got proper clothes and a place to hide out in Berlin, was another story.

After the meeting with GP I went up to the Unter den Linden and Friedrichstrasse to see the site of the 3rd Company's last battle. There I found our old reliable 'carts' knocked out, burned out and some of them overturned. Around them lay some bodies. They were my comrades, but they were all so burned or mutilated by grenades, that it was impossible to recognise any of them.

Everywhere there were still lots of destroyed German war material. The bodies of German soldiers were still lying in the streets some weeks after the end of the battle. Within days, all the thousands of Russian tanks that had been destroyed during the battle had been removed with feverish speed. No dead Bolsheviks could be seen on the streets. That was a sort of propaganda, too, and very efficient.

On 2 June, GP and I started our journey home. Equipped with blankets, a wash-bag from the Legation and a couple of blue-yellow armbands, we went up to the Fehrbelliner Platz early one morning, where we knew that the milk-transports to Nauen used to pass. As planned we could go with one of the carts. Shaking in the same rhythm as the milk bottles, we left Berlin.

In Nauen it was a big propaganda day as we arrived. Red flags were flying everywhere, and giant pictures of Stalin bordered the main street, where our cart was stopped by a traffic controller. Drums and martial music echoed, mixed with propaganda speeches and gramophone music from loudspeaker cars. The civil population kept a reserved distance. Not even the re-awakened local communists showed up. Perhaps they had made the same serious mistakes as the communists of Berlin. After the fall of the city they had taken out their old 'party' books from 1933 and their red armbands and beaming with joy went to meet the 'liberators.' But they were met with the violent blows of their proletarian brothers from Uzbekistan, Kazakhstan and other parts of the Red empire.

There were too many Red Army soldiers in Nauen to make us feel comfortable. We thanked the milkman for the ride and took the road to Hamburg. In Berlin we had heard that there was a transportation point across the Elbe in Wittenberge, and we intended to go there. Our first stopping place was called Selbelang. Near there we were offered a night's stay in a farmer's house. The farm was looted so much it was impossible to imagine. All the animals were gone and of the household utensils the farmer had hardly been allowed to keep the most necessary. The women in the house were hysterical. They had been raped. The farmer, still a convinced national socialist was happy that we were staying two days at the farm. GP and I acted as village 'doctors' with our wash-bag.

On the third day we said 'farewell' to the farmer's family and continued our wandering. We had got reinforcement! A 30 year-old woman joined us. She was on her way up towards Holstein, where she belonged. She no longer dared to walk alone and turned to us for protection. She was pregnant. Of course she was an inconvenient hanger-on, and slowed us down, but we could not leave the poor woman in trouble.

After having marched some kilometres with our 'ward,' we met a column of German soldiers guarded by some Red Army soldiers. The men in the column waved discretely but energetically at us to turn around. We knew why. Even before we left Selbelang, we had been warned about the next nearest big place. The name I do not remember any more, but here the Bolshevik's control had been especially hard. We went on despite that.

Some hundred metres further on we met a solitary cycling Russian, who observed us suspiciously and started to circle around us without a word. It started to get awkward and the woman showed signs of hysteria. To lighten the atmosphere GP finally approached the Russian and asked him for *mahorka*. The man was disarmed by GP's impudence, gave him a proper pinch of the brown moss and pedalled away. Now we had some tobacco again and did not have to collect butts from the road that tasted awful. Before we walked into the village we tidied ourselves, told the woman not to look so scared, and singing entered the lion's den.

Having reached the square, a group of Red Army soldiers, with murderous looks, turned up sure enough and showed signs of stopping us. We looked puzzled at them, raised our voices a little bit more, 'We wander over dew-sprinkled hills' echoed between the house walls, and we swung our arms in time with the song. The sons of the steppe watched us astonished and withdrew back to their vodka bottles in the former residence of the mayor.

At a quick march we left kilometre after kilometre behind us during our wandering towards the north-west. In an asparagus field we took a break for dinner and chewed fresh asparagus-tips. You can have worse food! As we were sitting there eating, two unpleasant figures came lumbering along, swarthy, ragged and dirty. They sat down by us and introduced themselves as Turks, recently let out from a concentration camp. They had killed one or two Germans who, according to them, had too much money. The woman moved a little bit closer to GP.

We told them that we were Swedes, but that did not mean much to them. I guess that studies about the country and people of Sweden do not take up much time in the schools in Turkey. Well, it was quite alright to dine with them at the field's edge, as long as you avoided looking at them. One single glance at their physiognomies was enough to transform the asparagus in your mouth to grass, dry as dust, and the swallowing function to get cramped! As soon as the right moment turned up, we said some kind words as 'goodbye', took our blankets and our ward between us, and wandered away.

As quarters for the night we chose a house whose interior looked as if it had been worked over with a chaff cutter. The Red Army never did anything by halves! Old, solid, rustic-style furniture, such as sofa beds, hundred year old cupboards, tables and chairs, with beautiful painting and ornament, had been transformed into firewood by nimble Bolsheviks. But we cleaned away the worst rubbish and rolled out our blankets. Then our friends the robber-murderers from the asparagus-field entered! The woman jumped up as if stung. GP, whom she had come to look upon as a sort of adoptive father, calmed her down. We took our blankets and moved out to the hay-loft in the barn across the yard. The night was quiet, and we were not disturbed by Turkish attempts to murder us. But for safety's sake GP and I alternately kept watch with a trusty parabellum at hand.

In the morning, as we climbed down to the yard, we were met by the almost idyllic sight of two quiet 'robber-murderers' cooking soup in the brittle light of the morning sun. They were in their best Turkish-morning-temper, and interrupted the soup cooking for a moment for a devout kneeling in the direction of Mecca. Then they rose and invited us to breakfast. We accepted and did not regret it afterwards. They certainly could cook! While we enjoyed the delicious onion and vegetable soup, our hosts handled the conversation, which mainly was about the brighter side of Mohammedan polygamy.

The woman showed hardly any appetite, but more signs of worry. Out of consideration for her we hurried up with our meal, quickly ate the soup, thanked the Turks and went off. Fortunately, it seemed that the woman had relatives in the surroundings and she wanted to stay there for a time. Probably it became too strenuous for her with the long marching distances. We handed her over safely and went on alone, but now with greater speed.

An ox-carriage caught up with us. It was the first time I had seen oxen running. There was a Bolshevik officer and an NCO sitting on the carriage. Insolent as always, GP stepped out in the middle of the road, stopped the equipage and asked them to pick us up. The officer grunted something inaudible and nodded. We jumped up and sat down close behind the officer. I had never before sat so close to a Russian officer – at least not a live one! As we sat there tilting to the steady but slow jog-trot of the oxen, the officer suddenly picked up a parabellum and started shooting wildly around him. At first we thought that he had gone crazy, but then understood that he was afraid of us and wanted to intimidate us with his weapon.

In the evening we arrived at Wittenberge. The whole day's journey had gone without any problems, thanks to travelling with the two Red Army soldiers. We went to see the commandant and applied for transportation across the Elbe. The answer was that we could come back 'some other time.'

In the square we met an armband-wearing, middle-aged fellow countrywoman from a Swedish textile city. She told us that we could share housing accommodation with her and another Swedish woman, married to a German, who also was waiting for a chance to get over. We followed her to the house, where a Russian major had been living until some days before, when he was involved in a car accident. Besides the two women there now were two Red Army NCOs, who were, I presumed, some sort of aides or servants to the major, because they guarded the boxes and suitcases that he had left behind.

For four days we stayed there waiting for the crossing. We spent the days strolling around in the town or standing by the river, looking over at the 'British' side. In the evenings, we sat at home with our two fellow countrywomen chatting till long after it had turned dark. We were told about the horror that had struck the 17-year old daughter of the woman we first met.

The mother had sent her daughter ahead, along with a German girl of the same age. On foot, they were on their way from Berlin to Wittenberge. A car with Russian officers had passed and at some distance the mother had seen the car stop right by the girls. They were pulled into the car that then drove away at high speed. Not until the next day did she find her daughter, who had totally broken down after being raped. Eventually the girl was sent into safety on the 'British' side.

During our evening conversations with the two Swedish women we compared our observations concerning the Russians. We agreed that they must be suffering from a deep feeling of inferiority in front of the Western people on whose ground they had set foot during the last days of the war. They could not have avoided comparing, despite the suffering of war, the better clothes, residential culture and higher living conditions, with the situation in their own country. It had to be this feeling of individual inferiority that caused their weird behaviour, which was now brutally cruel, now horribly ingratiating, now numbly irresolute, now spiteful. Our fellow countrywomen told us that the Russian major, who had been living in the house, one evening had told them what a deep impression it had made on him to see the difference of the woman's situation in Germany and in the Soviet Union.

"Russian woman so deep down, German woman so high up," he had said with distinct gestures to express the difference of social level.

The last evening, in our quarters in Wittenberge was interrupted in a very unpleasant way. The two servants had been looking askance at us ever since we first arrived. Perhaps it was jealousy. Before our arrival they too, in the evenings, had sat and chatted, although awkwardly, with the two women. But now they had been kept away. However, that evening at around eight o'clock, one of them came tramping down the stairs and into the kitchen. We all said "good evening" to him. He did not answer, but just moved around. He did not seem to have any real errand except to stare angrily at GP and me. Finally he went upstairs, after turning round in the door and sending a last, evil look in our direction. Five minutes later he came down again, now equipped with a uniform cap and submachine-gun. He went to the front door, turned to us and said:

"Komm, kamerrad, sprraechen!" ("Come, comrade, talk!")

GP asked what he wanted. We felt anything but comfortable. He looked completely wild.

"Komm sprraechen!" he repeated, now quite uncontrolled, and gestured at the door with his head.

There was nothing we could do. We nodded at the women, who had turned ghostly pale, and went out. It was pitch dark. GP tried to talk reasonably with the man, but it was hopeless. He shoved us in front of him and just said "Kommandantura!"

It was eerie to walk like this, in the dark, with an armed Red Army soldier behind us. Why, he could finish us off any minute! We were alert, ready to duck and overpower him. But nothing happened, and we arrived unhurt at the commandant's office. At the GPU department we were received by a good-looking Ukrainian girl, who spoke German fluently.

On a bed in the background a giant of a man lay snoring, with his muddy boots on a white bedspread. He was the GPU commander. Our supervisor did not let himself be put off by the woman, but demanded to talk to the commander. He was wakened by the talking and came to the table. Now our man started chattering. Through all the gabble we realised that he wanted us shot us as spies. The Ukrainian woman translated his dreary bunkum. GP immediately answered by showing our papers. He declared that we, who so far had got such a good opinion of the Red Army, unfortunately would have to change our view, if we were treated in this way.

It ended with the GPU commander telling the servant to go to hell, which he quickly did, apparently very confused. We left, with deep bows that the Ukrainian woman answered with coquettish and warm looks.

'Back home', we were received by two frightened and desperate women. They had believed that we were to be executed right away. That night we decided to keep watch with our weapons to hand.

In the morning, when we met the Swiss woman who managed the transports, she told us that the Russians had crossed out all Swedes and Swiss from the list of those who could cross the river that day. However, we made an agreement with her about another solution. This we hoped would work out all right, considering that the Bolsheviks, in the middle of their thorough searches, were often careless. Two Italians, who belonged to the permitted group of the day, had managed to cross the Elbe in some other way and now we planned to take their places. So that was how two Swedish lads, with not quite Mediterranean looks, boarded the ferry in the middle of a bunch of small, swarthy characters when a GPU officer down at the gate shouted: "Italians forward!"

Now, as we stepped on to the deck of the ferry and saw the bank with its GPU people and Red Army soldiers fade away, we thought, "We are almost home."

The feeling of having at long last got out of range of fire from the Red Army was overwhelming. We reached the other bank and were greeted by laughing British soldiers, with the words "Welcome back to civilisation!"

# Photographs

All photographs appear courtesy of Erik Norling. The publishers apologise for the poor quality of some of these images. However, due to their historical interest and rarity we have nevertheless decided to include them in this book.

Sven Olov Lindholm, founder of the "Lindholm movement" and leader of *Svensk Socialistik Samling* (Swedish Socialist Union), the organisation from which many of the Swedish Waffen-SS volunteers were drawn.

Swedish Waffen-SS volunteer.

*SS-Sturmmann* Patrik Mineur, the last of three brothers who were killed fighting
the Red Army. He was killed in action serving with 5th SS Panzer Division
'Wiking' in Poland, 13 October 1944.

Swedish SS officers Carl Svensson (foreground) and Gösta Borg (left rear),
spring 1944. Svensson was born in Hamburg, Germany, in 1915, and was a
graduate from the SS officers' school at Bad Tölz. Börg, likewise a graduate from
Bad Tölz, had served as a volunteer in Finland fighting the Russians. Both were
war correspondents by the time this image was taken.

Swedish *SS-Untersturmführer* Heino Meyer, twice reported killed in action.
Himmler personally cabled his condolences to Meyer's parents on two occasions.
Both times he turned up at his unit after periods in a field hospital.
Following the war he led a normal life in South America and Spain, with
unremovable shrapnel in his neck. Prior to his service in the *Panzer
Aufklärungs-Abteilung* of the 'Nordland' Division he had been a member of the
'Germania' Regiment, 'Wiking' Division.

Officers from the *Panzer Aufklärungs-Abteilung* of the 'Nordland' Division, Narva, 1944. *SS-Untersturmführer* Hans-Gösta Pehrsson is second from right.

Erik "Jerka" Wallin, the voice of this book, born 2 August 1921. He was a
member of Lindholm's party, and volunteered to fight Communism in 1939.
He did not see himself as any kind of hero, just a normal guy.

Hans-Gösta Pehrsson, the Swedish commander of the 3rd Company, *SS Panzer Aufklärungs-Abteilung* 11, 'Nordland' Division. Most of the Swedish SS volunteers served in this company. He ended the war with the rank of *SS-Hauptsturmführer*, and was the most decorated Swedish volunteer, having been awarded the Iron Cross 1st and 2nd class and *Ehrenblattspange*.

*SS-Sturmmann* Hans Linden, aged 17 years, and the first casualty amongst the Swedish volunteers, being killed in action in Russia on 27 December 1941.

*SS-Obersturmführer* Per Sigurd Baeklund, another Swedish SS volunteer,
who was awarded the Iron Cross 1st and 2nd class.

Gösta Borg, an officer at the front, later a war correspondent.

A SdKfz 250 armoured personnel carrier belonging to the 4th Company, *Panzer Aufklärungs-Abteilung* 11. Note the 'sun wheel', a modified swastika, a pre-Christian Nordic symbol adopted by the 'Nordland' Division. The 'sun wheel' appears on many rune stones erected in Scandinavia as chronicles chiselled in granite of important events and personalities before the – frequently violent – conversion to Christianity in the 11th century. Some pagan customs and rites are still alive in the Nordic countries.

Troops from 'Nordland' Division, Courland, late 1944.

A drawing of Swedish SS volunteers by Finn Wigforss, a war artist who served with the 'Wiking' Division.

Finnish-Swedish volunteer Ola Olin.

The last known image of Swedish participation in the Battle of Berlin – a
knocked-out armoured personnel carrier from the 'Nordland' Division
(note sun wheel insignia), May 1945. The body lying to the right of
the vehicle appears to be Swede Ragnar Johansson, the unit's last casualty.

# Appendix I

# Felix Steiner

Felix Steiner was born on 23 May 1896 in Ebensrode, in East Prussia. He volunteered as an officer candidate with the 5th Infantry Regiment 'Von Boyen' in Tilsit, in March 1914.

By the time the First World War broke out, he had advanced to 2nd Lieutenant and went to the front with his regiment. He was badly wounded and was awarded the Iron Cross 2nd Class for bravery.

After recovering and being fit to fight again, Steiner was transferred to a machine-gun unit and was sent to the Courland Front, where he later was awarded the Iron Cross 1st Class. In October 1918 he was promoted to 1st Lieutenant.

A short time after the armistice of Germany in November 1918, he joined one of the many Freikorps and participated in the fighting in the Memelland, particularly in Königsberg. In 1921 Felix Steiner became an active officer and in 1922 he successfully passed the General Staff examination.

In 1933, he became a *Major*. Steiner was transferred to the SS in March 1935, as an *SS-Obersturmbannführer*. He was then appointed commander of the 1st Battalion of the SS Regiment 'Deutschland' and in 1936 he was promoted to *SS-Standartenführer* and commander of the same Regiment in Munich.

Felix Steiner was a very ambitious and skilful educator and organiser. He contributed greatly to this Regiment's later successes at the Front. He participated in the Polish Campaign in 1939 and in the Western Campaign in 1940. As a result, on 15 August 1940 he was awarded the Knight's Cross of the Iron Cross. On 9 September the same year he was promoted to *SS-Brigadeführer* and Major-General of the Waffen-SS.

He successfully participated in shaping the 5th SS Division Wiking, which he was to command on the Eastern Front 1941–1943. He was particularly successful in forming units consisting of foreign volunteers. In his case these units consisted of Dutch, Danes, Norwegians, Finns and Swedes.

He was fully aware that he had to deal with different national mentalities, and that it was not always possible to train them in exactly the same way as if they were Germans. Among other things, Steiner drummed into his officers that they should take into consideration the different backgrounds and temperaments of the volunteers, and take positive advantage of the differences.

He was very demanding and maintained strict discipline and order. "If you turn a blind eye to punishable deeds, the unit will be weakened, the morale will sink, the discipline disintegrate, the fighting power and the soldiers respect for other humans, will deteriorate. With this as background, I reserve to myself the right to court-martial anyone who commits a crime against the inhabitants of a country." (In that instance he meant Soviet citizens.)

On 23 December 1942 he was awarded the Oak Leaves to the Knight's Cross. He had now advanced to *SS-Gruppenführer* and Lieutenant-General of the Waffen-SS.

On 31 March 1943 Felix Steiner was given responsibility for the creation of the III (Germanic) *SS-Panzerkorps*, which consisted of the 11th SS Division Nordland and the 23rd SS Division Nederland. Both of these were *Panzergrenadier* divisions.

Under the firm command of Steiner the two divisions were welded together into an élite unit of a unique type.

Later the 28th SS *Panzergrenadier* Division Wallonie was also put under his command. On 10 August 1944 Steiner was awarded the Swords to the Knight's Cross, thanks to the successes of his *Panzerkorps*. During the formation of the *Panzerkorps* he had been promoted to *SS-Obergruppenführer* and General of the Waffen-SS.

At the end of January 1945 the defence of Pomerania fell to Steiner's lot. He was also chosen to be commander of the 11th SS *Panzerarmee*.

On 3 May 1945, Felix Steiner went into captivity with his men. The victors did their utmost to find something with which to accuse him of war crimes, but failed. Along with most of his army colleagues, Steiner was cleared. The same also went for his divisions. This, however, did not prevent the victors from keeping this man of honour in prison for three years, and not until 27 April 1948 was he set free.

At the US Military Academy in West Point hangs a large oil painting of SS-General Felix Steiner, respected and admired by his former enemies.

On 12 May 1966 Felix Steiner died at his home in Munich. Thousands of his old soldiers attended his funeral. With him died one of the great personalities of the Second World War.

# Appendix II

# Waffen-SS Ranks

| | |
|---|---|
| *SS-Schütze/SS-Panzergrenadier* | Private |
| *SS-Oberschütze* | Senior Private (after 6 months service) /Private 1st Class |
| *SS-Sturmmann* | Lance-Corporal |
| *SS-Rottenführer* | Senior Lance-Corporal |
| *SS-Unterscharführer* | Corporal |
| *SS-Scharführer* | Sergeant |
| *SS-Oberscharführer* | Senior Sergeant |
| *SS-Hauptscharführer* | Sergeant-Major |
| *SS-Sturmscharführer* | Staff Sergeant (after 15 years service) |
| *SS-Junker* | Officer candidate with substantive rank of *SS-Unterscharführer* |
| *SS-Standartenjunker* | Officer candidate with substantive rank of *SS-Scharführer* |
| *SS-Standartenoberjunker* | Officer candidate with substantive rank of *SS-Hauptscharführer* |
| *SS-Untersturmführer* | Second Lieutenant |
| *SS-Obersturmführer* | First Lieutenant |
| *SS-Hauptsturmführer* | Captain |
| *SS-Sturmbannführer* | Major |
| *SS-Obersturmbannführer* | Lieutenant-Colonel |
| *SS-Standartenführer* | Colonel |
| *SS-Oberführer* | Brigadier |
| *SS-Brigadeführer* | Major-General |
| *SS-Gruppenführer* | Lieutenant-General |
| *SS-Obergruppenführer* | General |
| *SS-Oberstgruppenführer* | General |
| *Reichsführer-SS* | Supreme Commander of the SS – Heinrich Himmler |

# Appendix III

# Organisation of SS *Panzer Aufklärungs Abteilung* 11

The *Panzer Aufklärungs Abteilung* of 11th SS *Panzergrenadier* Division Nordland consisted of six companies in total – a staff company and five reconnaissance companies.

*Staff company*

Equipped with light and medium armoured personnel carriers. The Signals Platoon included seven 80-watt radios and 2 telephones; the Orderly Platoon was equipped with 15 *Schwimmwagen*.

*1st Company*

| | |
|---|---|
| 1st Platoon | 6 eight-wheeled heavy armoured cars, 4 with 2cm gun and MG each, 2 with 80-watt radio sets |
| 2nd Platoon | 6 four-wheeled armoured cars, 4 with 2cm gun and MG 42 each, 2 with 80-watt radio sets |
| 3rd Platoon | As 2nd Platoon |
| 4th Platoon | As 2nd Platoon |

*2nd Company*

| | |
|---|---|
| 1st Platoon | 4 SdKfz 250/9 turreted half-tracks with 2cm guns and MGs, 2 radio APCs |
| 2nd Platoon | As 1st Platoon |
| 3rd Platoon | As 1st Platoon |
| 4th Platoon | As 1st Platoon |

*3rd Company ('The Swedish Company')*

3 light platoons each of 3 sections, equipped principally with SdKfz 250/1 half-tracks. The 4th (Heavy) Platoon contained SdKfz 250/7 half-tracks armed with 8cm mortars. Known to the men as 'The Swedish Company', as it was in this unit in which the majority of the Swedes served. It was commanded for much of its existence by *SS-Untersturmführer* Hans-Gösta Pehrsson (referred to as 'GP' by Wallin).

*4th Company*

As 3rd Company.

*5th (Heavy) Company*

1st Platoon    4 SdKfz 251/1 half-tracks towing 7.5cm PAK
2nd Platoon    2 SdKfz 251/1 half-tracks towing 7.5cm infantry guns
3rd Platoon    3 engineer sections equipped with SdKfz 251/7
                half-tracks, including flamethrowers, bridge-laying
                equipment and inflatable boats.
4th Platoon    6 SdKfz 251/9 half-tracks armed with 7.5cm PAK

In total the fully equipped *Abteilung* numbered about 800 men, divided into 120 men in each reconnaissance company and 200 men in the staff company. However, as with all late-war German formations, casualties were very high and the unit was seldom, if ever, at full strength.

# Related titles published by Helion & Company

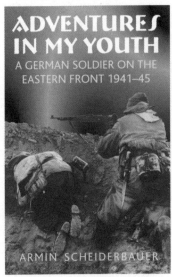
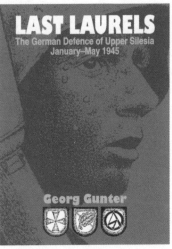